Windows 11 for Seniors: 2022 Complete Guide to Master Windows 11 OS. Screenshots, the Best Tips&Tricks, and Simple Explanations Included

Copyright © 2022

All rights reserved.

ISBN:9798847018623

© **Copyright 2022 - All rights reserved.**

The content contained within this book may not be reproduced, duplicated, or transmitted without direct written permission from the author or the publisher.

Under no circumstances will any blame or legal responsibility be held against the publisher, or author, for any damages, reparation, or monetary loss due to the information contained within this book. Either directly or indirectly. You are responsible for your own choices, actions, and results.

Legal Notice:

This book is copyright protected. This book is only for personal use. You cannot amend, distribute, sell, use, quote, or paraphrase any part, or the content within this book, without the consent of the author or publisher.

Disclaimer Notice:

Please note the information contained within this document is for educational and entertainment purposes only. All effort has been executed to present accurate, up-to-date, and reliable, complete information. No warranties of any kind are declared or implied. Readers acknowledge that the author is not engaging in the rendering of legal, financial, medical, or professional advice. The content within this book has been derived from various sources. Please consult a licensed professional before attempting any techniques outlined in this book.

By reading this document, the reader agrees that under no circumstances is the author responsible for any losses, direct or indirect, which are incurred as a result of the use of the information contained within this document, including, but not limited to, — errors, omissions, or inaccuracies.

CONTENTS:

Introduction — 7

Chapter 1: Basic information to use your PC. — 9

    When to Use the Computer's Power Button — 10

    How to Make a Computer Shutdown — 11

    How to Power Off a Device Without the Power Button — 12

    How to Change the Function of the Power Button — 13

    How to use mouse and keyboard — 14

Chapter 2: Windows 11 — 22

    What is Windows 11? — 22

    Why use Windows 11? — 25

    How to find Settings in Windows 11 — 29

    How to Use Windows 11 New Settings? — 31

Chapter 3: How to work with files and documents — 37

    About files and folders — 37

    Microsoft Word — 44

Chapter 4: About the Internet — 49

    Seniors' Access to the Internet and Technical Jargon — 49

    Seniors' Guide to Search Engines — 52

    Keeping Seniors Safe Online — 55

    Resources and Websites — 59

Chapter 5: Communication with family and Friends   **62**

    Gmail   63

    WhatsApp   68

    Viber   72

Chapter 6: What are shortcuts?   **76**

    The most popular shortcuts   76

    Advanced shortcuts   81

    Additional standard keyboard shortcuts in Windows 11   86

Conclusion   **89**

Windows 11 for Seniors

Introduction

It is a widely held belief that elderly people are often technophobic and unwilling to learn how to use computers, although this is not totally accurate. Increasing numbers of seniors are realizing how advantageous it would be to have a computer at home. They may still want assistance in selecting and utilizing a computer, but the benefits will be well worth the effort.

The elderly can accept new technologies.

Getting Started

The computer must be user-friendly. The mouse on a desktop computer is frequently easier to operate than that on a laptop; but, a laptop or tablet offer a transportable alternative. Those who are comfortable with typewriters may prefer a conventional keyboard, although touch displays may be suitable for others. Shop around for the most appropriate broadband bundle based on expected consumption.

Everyone needs assistance in mastering the fundamentals. At school, children are taught how to use computers, but adults will not have had this chance. People over the age of 65 who did not use a computer throughout their working years may have little or no computer skills. Friends or relatives may be able to help someone get started and provide training. Alternatively, several introductory computer classes are offered at local adult education centers.

Benefits

The Internet offers so much to offer seniors, from health and lifestyle information to hobbies and recipes. There is quick access to news and weather predictions as well as telephone contact information online at all times (who knows the number for directory inquiries these days?)

Shopping

Particularly for elderly individuals with limited mobility, standing in checkout lines and lugging big bags of groceries is a chore. People may order groceries and other items to be delivered to their door using a computer. If desired, several large grocery chains will even deliver your groceries to your kitchen.

Social Contact

Currently, the fastest-growing demographic on Facebook is adults over 65. Email, Skype, and photo sharing are good methods for preventing elderly loneliness. A distant relative might nonetheless feel included in the life of his or her family through video conversations and online correspondence.

Maintaining Mental Agility

Distance learning classes are an excellent approach to stimulate the mind. Some researchers are even beginning to investigate the cognitive advantages of some computer games for elderly individuals.

When it comes to technology, older individuals are proving that they are fully capable of acquiring computer literacy if they so want. A little assistance from relatives or friends is sufficient to get started.

So as you can see, computers may be very useful for seniors and my book was created to help them understand PC and how it works better. I will try to avoid the too hard topics that are not interesting for seniors. Here I will discover the basic things that to begin

.

Chapter 1: Basic information to use your PC.

The power button is a round or square button that turns on and off an electrical gadget. Almost every electrical equipment has a power button or switch.

Typically, the gadget turns on when the button is pressed and off when it is pressed again.

A hard power button is mechanical; when pressed, you can feel a click and typically see a difference in depth between the on and off positions. The far more popular soft power button is electrical and appears identical while the gadget is on and off.

Some older gadgets include a power switch that functions similarly to a physical power button. A flip of the switch in one way activates the gadget, while a flip in the opposite direction deactivates it.

Symbols for Power Button On/Off (I & O)

Typically, power buttons and switches are marked with "I" and "O" symbols.

The "I" signifies power on while the "O" signifies power off. This identification is occasionally I/O or the "I" and "O" characters stacked as a single character, as shown in the photography

Power Button Locations on Computers

There are power buttons on many types of computers, including desktops, tablets, netbooks, and laptops. They are often located on the side or top of mobile devices, or sometimes adjacent to the keyboard, if present.

In a conventional desktop computer configuration, power buttons and switches are located on the front and occasionally the back of the display, as well as on the front and back of the computer cabinet. The power button on the rear of the chassis controls the power supply.

When to Use the Computer's Power Button

The optimal time to shut down a computer is when all software programs have been closed and work has been saved. However, it is preferable to utilize the operating system's shutdown procedure.

If your computer is no longer responding to your mouse or keyboard inputs, you may wish to switch it off by pressing the power button. Using the actual power button to shut down the computer is likely the best course of action in this scenario.

Please note, however, that if you force your computer to shut down, all open applications and files will be terminated without warning. Not only will you lose your current work, but you may also corrupt certain files.

Depending on the corrupted files, your computer may be unable to restart.

The act of pressing the power button Once

It may seem rational to push the power button once to shut off a computer, but this seldom works, especially on computers produced in this century (i.e., the vast majority!).

One of the benefits of soft power buttons, as we covered in the introduction, is that users may set them to do multiple actions due to their electrical nature and direct computer communication.

If the computer is functioning properly, most computers are configured to sleep or hibernate when the power button is pressed.

If a single push does not compel your computer to shut down (which is quite likely), you will need to try something different.

How to Make a Computer Shutdown

If you have no other option but to force the computer to shut down, you may often hold down the power button until the machine no longer displays any indications of life; the screen will turn black, all the lights should go out, and the computer should stop making noises.

Once the computer is turned off, the same power button may be used to turn it back on. This form of restart is referred to as a hard reset or hard reboot.

How to Power Off a Device Without the Power Button

If possible, avoid just turning off your computer or other device. It is never a good idea to terminate ongoing processes on your computer, smartphone, or other device without first alerting the operating system, for the reasons you have just seen.

A computer may need to be turned off or restarted without using the power button if the button is faulty and will not function as intended. It may occur on both smartphones and PCs.

How to Restart Your Computer? Right-clicking the Start button brings up a long list of shortcuts, towards the bottom of which is "Shut down or sign out." Mouse over that option and then click "Shut down." Even while this still requires two clicks (plus a mouse-over).

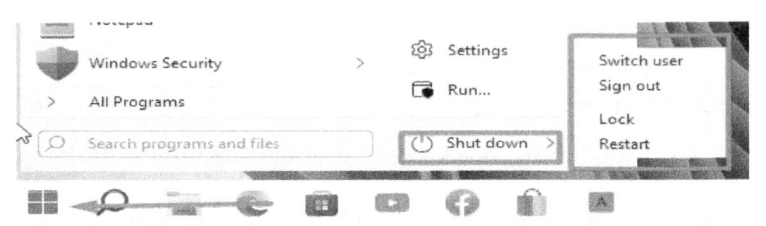

Additional Information on Device Power-Off

Typically, a software-based mechanism is provided to switch off a device, however this is not always the case. Some devices' shutdown is initiated by the power button, but completed by the device's operating system.

Smartphones are the most prominent example. The majority of devices need you to hold down the power button until the software prompts you to confirm that you intend to switch off the device. Obviously, certain devices, such as a computer monitor, do not run an operating system and may be safely shut off by pushing the power button once.

How to Change the Function of the Power Button

Windows has a built-in option for customizing the behavior of the power button.

1. Open Control Panel.
2. Proceed to the Hardware and Sound area. Windows 11 calls it Printers and Other Hardware. (Don't see it? If you're seeing a Control Panel with icons instead of categories, you may continue forward to Step 3.)

3. Select Power Options.

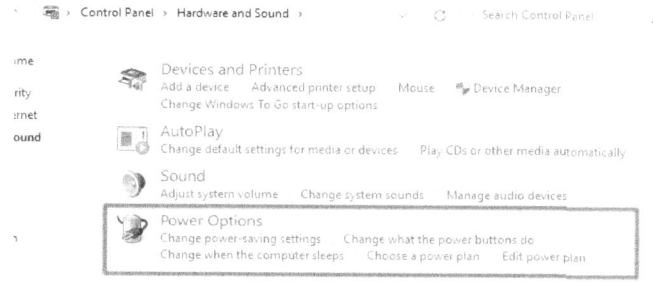

4. Select from the left. Depending on the Windows version, choose what the power buttons do or choose what the power button does.

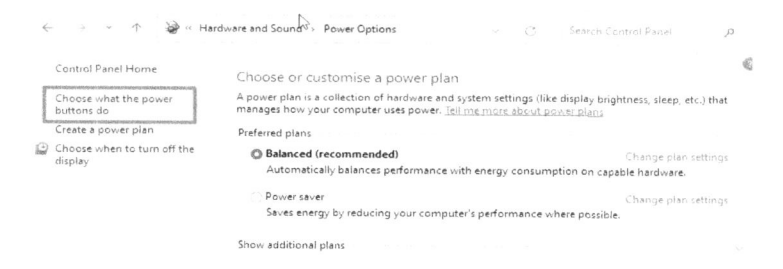

5. Select a menu item next to When I click the power button:. It may be None, Sleep, Hibernate, or Shut down. In some configurations, you may also see Display off.

Windows 11 for Seniors

[Screenshot showing Power Options > System Settings dialog with "Define power buttons and turn on password protection", power and sleep button settings dropdown showing "Do nothing / Shut down / Turn off the display", and Shut-down settings with Lock option.]

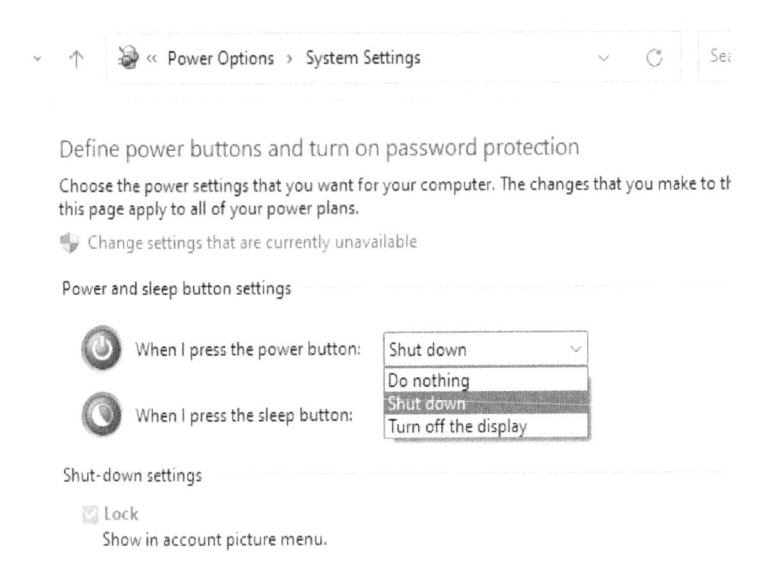

6. When you have finished modifying the power button's function, choose Save changes or OK.

Well done, now you know how to turn on/off your computer. Go to the next step!

How to use mouse and keyboard

How to use mouse

With the help of your computer mouse, you can move the cursor (pointer) around the screen and then "click" to launch a program, start typing somewhere specific, or access a menu of options. If you don't like the laptop's built-in touchpad, you can use a desktop computer's mouse instead, which is what every desktop computer has.

The computer mouse, created in 1963 by Douglas Engelbart, has evolved over time and now comes in a variety of styles. It is known as a "mouse" because of its basic mouse-like shape and the tail-like appearance of the wire that connects it to the computer. According to the Oxford English Dictionary, "mice" and "mouses" are both acceptable plural nouns for the device.

To specify direction, mice were first created using two gear wheels, and then with a "trackball" that moved in contact with a surface. These days, optical mice that detect direction by light are more prevalent. Mice can also be cordless, which makes moving them simpler.

Learn how to use your mouse by adhering to these detailed instructions.

- Pick up your mouse and examine it in the first step.
- There are two buttons at the front, left and right, that point away from you. You press these, or more accurately, "click" these to activate the action.
- The majority of mouse also have a wheel between the buttons that you may roll to scroll up and down the screen.
- Acquire a comfortable mouse grip. It is typically held in this manner, between your thumb and little finger:
- Press a button. Click the left button with your index finger, then the right button with your middle finger:
- Use the opposing fingers if you are left-handed. To alter which buttons do what, you can often change your computer's options.
- Try a double-click in step four. On the left button, this occurs pretty frequently. The second click must be made as promptly as feasible. A particular "window" is identified by the first click, and a button, link, or other item is chosen to perform an action in that window by the second click. Click rapidly; if you click too slowly, the computer will assume that you are repeatedly telling it where you are.
- Practice is now necessary. On the PCP Library website, you can discover several straightforward mouse drills. Place the pointer over the highlighted "basic mouse exercises" above (this is referred to as a "link") and press the left button to access them from here. Did you notice that when the cursor was over the link, it changed into a tiny hand? This indicates that you can click on that word or phrase to navigate to another page on that website or the entire internet.

- Now try a right-click in step six. Pay no attention to where the cursor is located on the screen; simply click the right button. Options will be presented to you in a menu. Right-clicking always brings up a menu. The menu will close if you move your cursor outside of it and then left-click.
- You'll frequently be instructed to "click," as well as occasionally to "double-click" or "triple-click." It always means to press the left button when it says this. If you need to "right-click," you will always be instructed to do so!

Done!

How to use your keyboard?

A "QWERTY" keyboard is the most popular type of keyboard, named for the keys on the top row of letters. When figuring out where the keys of a manual typewriter should be placed, C. L. Scholes created it in the 1860s.

Learn how to use your keyboard by following these detailed instructions.

You must have a document open that you can type into in order to complete the straightforward activities below.

Step 1: Carefully examine your keyboard. The figure below labels the keys that are the most significant:

Some keyboards have a somewhat varied layout, particularly those on laptops. Yours, for instance, might not have a number pad or have the delete key in a different location. But these significant keys will be

To specify direction, mice were first created using two gear wheels, and then with a "trackball" that moved in contact with a surface. These days, optical mice that detect direction by light are more prevalent. Mice can also be cordless, which makes moving them simpler.

Learn how to use your mouse by adhering to these detailed instructions.

- Pick up your mouse and examine it in the first step.
- There are two buttons at the front, left and right, that point away from you. You press these, or more accurately, "click" these to activate the action.
- The majority of mouse also have a wheel between the buttons that you may roll to scroll up and down the screen.
- Acquire a comfortable mouse grip. It is typically held in this manner, between your thumb and little finger:
- Press a button. Click the left button with your index finger, then the right button with your middle finger:
- Use the opposing fingers if you are left-handed. To alter which buttons do what, you can often change your computer's options.
- Try a double-click in step four. On the left button, this occurs pretty frequently. The second click must be made as promptly as feasible. A particular "window" is identified by the first click, and a button, link, or other item is chosen to perform an action in that window by the second click. Click rapidly; if you click too slowly, the computer will assume that you are repeatedly telling it where you are.
- Practice is now necessary. On the PCP Library website, you can discover several straightforward mouse drills. Place the pointer over the highlighted "basic mouse exercises" above (this is referred to as a "link") and press the left button to access them from here. Did you notice that when the cursor was over the link, it changed into a tiny hand? This indicates that you can click on that word or phrase to navigate to another page on that website or the entire internet.

- Now try a right-click in step six. Pay no attention to where the cursor is located on the screen; simply click the right button. Options will be presented to you in a menu. Right-clicking always brings up a menu. The menu will close if you move your cursor outside of it and then left-click.
- You'll frequently be instructed to "click," as well as occasionally to "double-click" or "triple-click." It always means to press the left button when it says this. If you need to "right-click," you will always be instructed to do so!

Done!

How to use your keyboard?

A "QWERTY" keyboard is the most popular type of keyboard, named for the keys on the top row of letters. When figuring out where the keys of a manual typewriter should be placed, C. L. Scholes created it in the 1860s.

Learn how to use your keyboard by following these detailed instructions.

You must have a document open that you can type into in order to complete the straightforward activities below.

Step 1: Carefully examine your keyboard. The figure below labels the keys that are the most significant:

Some keyboards have a somewhat varied layout, particularly those on laptops. Yours, for instance, might not have a number pad or have the delete key in a different location. But these significant keys will be located somewhere on almost every keyboard.

Step 2: The letter keys serve as the primary keys. You get lower-case print when you only type with these. However, if you simultaneously hold down one of the two "shift keys" (there are two to select from), you will text in UPPER-CASE letters.

Put your name in capital letters (UPPER-CASE) and with spaces. The broad key at the bottom of the keyboard is the "space bar," which you push briefly to make a space.

Step 3: There is always a fix if you type something incorrectly.

Place your cursor (mouse pointer) exactly behind the letter and click to erase it. then momentarily press Backspace. (Always push quickly; if you don't, you'll get lots of repeated omissions, spaces, letters, etc.) Alternately, position your cursor immediately prior to the letter, click, and then press Delete.

Step 4: Attempt to type a sentence now.

Given that it uses the majority of the alphabetic letters, this sentence is a good one to practice writing.

Step 5: Using the arrow keys, you can move the pointer along this sentence without destroying anything:

Windows 11 for Seniors

Try advancing and reversing the cursor through your statement.

Step 6: If you have a number pad, try using it now.

You must press the Num Lock key in order to utilize this to input numbers. To indicate that it is on, there may be an indicator light at the top of the keyboard or on the "Num Lock" key itself.

Step 7: The primary keyboard's numbers are another option for typing. They are located on the row of keys above the first row of letters.

There are numerous symbols, such as "£," "&," and "!" above these numbers. Hold down the Shift key as you type to use them. Thus, pressing the number 7 alone results in the letter "7," whereas pressing the number 7 while holding down the "Shift" key results in the letter "&."

Similar extra symbols can be found on the keyboard in other places:

They function in the same manner as the ones that are above the numbers.

Step 8: Press the Caps Lock key and input the following if you want everything to be in capital letters:

Once more, an indicator light can illuminate to indicate that your capitals are "locked." Don't forget to hit this key once more to turn off "Caps Lock" when you're done.

Step 9: The "Windows" key is available in a variety of styles, such as the one seen in the picture

It performs the exact same function as the Windows button on your computer's taskbar. By pressing this key or by using the mouse to click the taskbar button, you can select to launch the "Start" menu.

Step 10: There are many different ways to navigate a web page. To see where they lead you, try using the following keys: For some actions, you'll be instructed to use the Control (Ctrl) and Alternate (Alt) keys. Keep pressing any other keys while continuing to hold down one or both of the keys.

For instance, if you simultaneously hit Ctrl, Alt, and Delete, a menu will appear. Press the Escape (Esc) key in the upper left corner of the keyboard to make it disappear.

Step 11: Keyboard shortcuts can be used to do some mouse-related tasks. These frequently entail using the "Ctrl" and/or "Alt" keys and call for holding down one key while pushing another. Some individuals favor using them over the mouse.

Chapter 2: Windows 11

What is Windows 11?

Microsoft's most recent desktop OS is called Windows 11. Windows 10 had been billed as "the last version of Windows," therefore few people were expecting it to debut until early 2021.

People all throughout the world were reliant on Microsoft's products during the epidemic, whether it was for distant work or just to stay in touch with loved ones. Given the apparent longevity of these emerging styles, the corporation has opted to start over.

Windows 11 is a radical redesign that emphasizes cleanliness and ease of use. Windows 10X, an aborted fork of Windows 10 optimized for touchscreen devices, serves as inspiration for several features. Microsoft seems determined at the moment to make Windows 11 a fantastic operating system for a wide range of hardware configurations.

It is now possible to install Windows 11 on all compatible laptops and PCs by going to Settings or downloading and installing it manually. In 2022, practically all laptops, outside of Macs and Chromebooks, will be powered by Windows 11.

Despite its apparent simplicity, Windows 11 has a wide variety of features, many of which are interesting enough to warrant further investigation. The purpose of this comprehensive guide is to provide you with the information you need to get the most out of your Windows 11 experience.

Windows 11, which Microsoft had announced was being released on October 5, 2021, was really released on that day.

When was just the day that original equipment manufacturers (OEMs) could start releasing devices running Windows 11. The upgrade will be made available to "in-market devices" that meet the requirements in a staggered and measured rollout, according to the blog post.

But a January 2022 blog post from the company's official blog stated that this was indeed ahead of time. As of this writing, Windows 11 has entered "its last phase of availability," meaning all remaining devices should get the upgrade very soon if they haven't already.

However, you may access it immediately without waiting for delivery to your computer. A final version may be downloaded from Microsoft's site if you're okay with performing the installation process by hand. If you wish to install from a USB drive, you should use this ISO file instead.

You mean Windows 10 is the last one?

At least, that's what Microsoft claimed when it unveiled Windows 10. But it looks like it's had a change of heart. The business may have gambled that its users would quickly forget that it had previously promised these changes in a Windows 10 update by not bringing it up during the launch event.

Interestingly, this was discussed during a Microsoft hybrid workplace event in April of 2022. However, the pandemic was cited as the primary reason for this shift in strategy, with the corporation noting that "how, when, and where we operate profoundly altered overnight."

Windows 11 require:

- Speedy dual-core CPU,
- 4GB of RAM, and 64GB of storage space at 1GHz
- Supports UEFI and Secure Boot
- Certified Module for Reliable Platforms (TPM) Display greater than 9 inches, 720p or higher resolution DirectX 12 graphics card
- Access to the web and a Microsoft account

Not sure if it will work with your gadget? Microsoft's free "PC Health Check" program is intended to accomplish precisely that. You may get it at the very bottom of Microsoft's Windows 11 download page.

If data storage experts Trendfocus (via Tom's Hardware) are to be believed, this storage need might become SSD-only by 2023. Hard disk drive (HDD) and embedded multi-media card (eMMC) based Windows 11 devices are not likely to be impacted.

The installation of Windows 11 on incompatible hardware is not recommended by Microsoft, although it is possible. In all likelihood, you will be presented with messages in Settings and on the desktop indicating that your device is incompatible. However, it doesn't appear to have any impact on speed or app compatibility.

In June of 2022, the business made the mistake of releasing the 22H2 feature upgrade to unsupported Windows 10 devices. The same caveats as before apply: only test this out if you have a secondary Windows 10 device hanging around, not on your primary PC.

Why use Windows 11?

Windows 11 has some new features that can become a reason to use this OS.

There are far too many for me to list them all, but here are the most important ones.

The most obvious change is the extensive cosmetic one. Windows 11 will be a major departure from Windows 10, which has had a consistent design throughout its lifetime.

The new taskbar rearranges the icons so that they are in the middle, although the old arrangement may be restored with a click. However, Microsoft is working to restore some of the features it cut from Windows 7 in favor of Windows 10. The time and date will be displayed on all external displays after the upgrade in February 2022, and the 22H2 feature update is scheduled to bring back drag-and-drop functionality.

There aren't any major drawbacks to the new Start Menu, but its unconventional layout won't appeal to everyone. In fact, this design approach is reminiscent of what Microsoft previewed for Windows 10X, which was ultimately scrapped.

It contains a grid of adjustable 'Pinned' icons, plus separate 'All apps' area for whatever else you have installed. The 'Recommended' section below displays frequently used files, programs and folders – including from cloud services such as OneDrive and Microsoft 365 – enabling you to easily pick up where you left off, even if you last used a different device.

However, many individuals have been dissatisfied by this, notably the lack of customizing flexibility. However, Microsoft has recently provided the opportunity to alter the split between Pinned and Recommended parts.

Snap Layouts, a new multitasking tool, has been favorably received. How to find it you can see in the image below, the app layout may be customized by hovering over the maximize button.

System > Multi-tasking

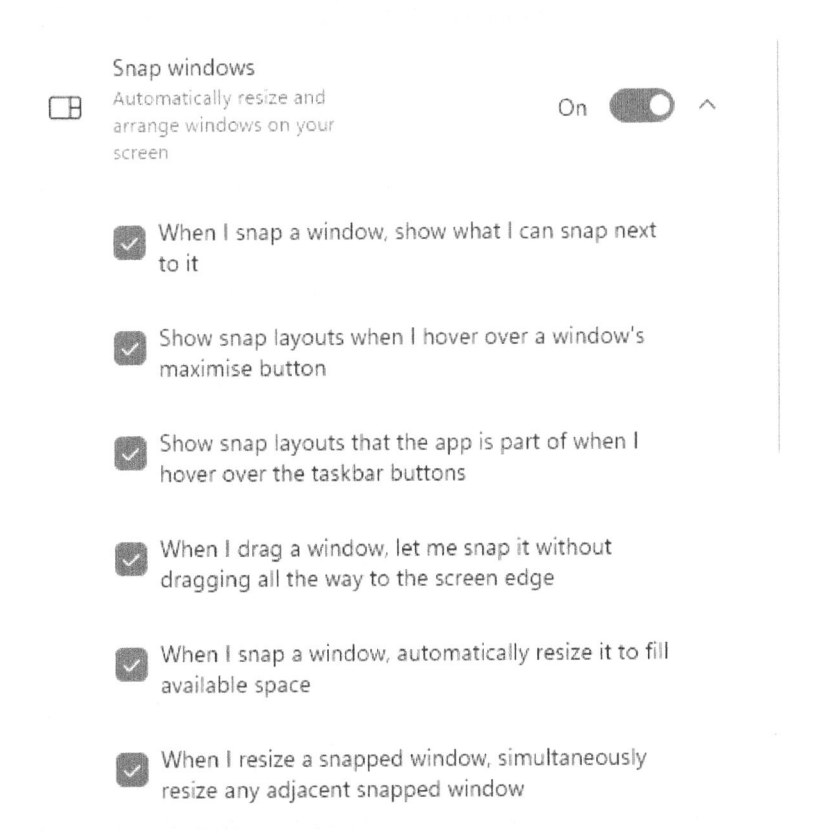

Snap windows
Automatically resize and arrange windows on your screen — On

- ✓ When I snap a window, show what I can snap next to it
- ✓ Show snap layouts when I hover over a window's maximise button
- ✓ Show snap layouts that the app is part of when I hover over the taskbar buttons
- ✓ When I drag a window, let me snap it without dragging all the way to the screen edge
- ✓ When I snap a window, automatically resize it to fill available space
- ✓ When I resize a snapped window, simultaneously resize any adjacent snapped window

Up until now, widgets haven't played a significant role in Windows releases, but that's changing. The panel appears from the left side of the screen by default, but it may be resized to take up the entire display if desired. It's made to be opened and read quickly, with only a few key points highlighted, without requiring you to stop what you're doing.

Notifications may now be triggered from the taskbar's weather and stock widgets. According to a report by The Verge, moving icons will soon replace previously static ones. If, for example, a rainstorm is approaching or your preferred stocks begin trading lower, you will be given a more blatant warning. Some users may find this annoying, but there is currently no clear method to disable it. Microsoft provides further information on Widgets in a support article.

Other than that, the chat feature of Microsoft Teams is now included right into Windows 11, and in the future, you'll be able to do things like share windows and mute calls from the taskbar itself:

The Edge web browser is now integrated with Teams, so you can view open tabs in Task Manager. During incognito sessions, Edge tabs on the taskbar will display a generic icon instead of the site, icon, and topic name.

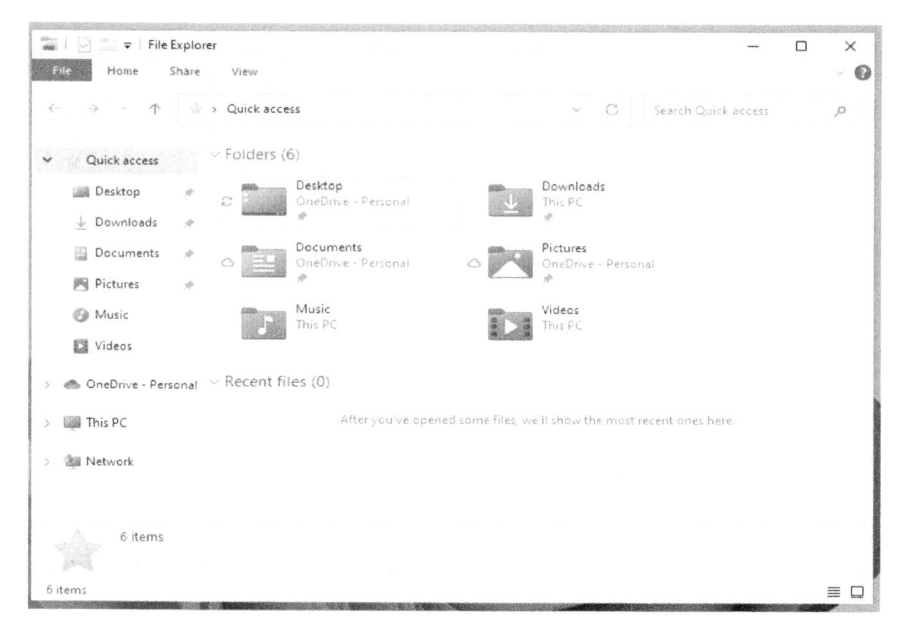

Both File Explorer and the Microsoft Store are only two of the many preinstalled programs that have been updated. This second option allows you to use the Epic Games Store or any other Android app available on the Amazon Appstore. There is currently no evidence to suggest the Google Play Store will be included into Windows 11, however a workaround does exist.

However, Google is developing a specialized Play Store Games app in case you choose to stick with official services. This should be launched before the year 2022 and be backwards-compatible with Windows 11 and Windows 10.

The new Action Center in Windows 11 divides Quick Settings, Notifications, and a music controller into their own tabs. Its user-friendly layout, modeled after Windows 10X, enables effortless navigation with a touchpad, mouse, stylus, or finger.

Windows 11 also has a new Snipping Tool. It replaces Windows 10's Snip & Sketch, but offers a lot more functionality than the legacy Snipping Tool found on earlier iterations of Windows.

Plenty of stock apps have also been redesigned to be more in keeping with Windows 11's new design. They include Calculator, Clock, Notepad, Media Player and File Explorer, with the latter shown below:

A new volume gauge has been introduced, nine years after the last one debuted. What to anticipate is as follows.

This is intended to look and feel like the rest of the Windows 11 user interface. It has both light and dark themes, with the same brightness sliders accessible through shortcuts. The Your Phone companion app now has a window for calls that are already in process, there are additional themes available for the on-screen keyboard, and the clock may be removed.

The Edge web browser now supports the Microsoft Teams integration, which has met with mixed reviews. This allows Task Manager to have many tabs, each of which displays different information (such as GPU or crashpad data). If you're not using private browsing mode, the tabs on your taskbar will display the site, icon, and subject name.

Since February 2022, editions of Task Manager have included an "Eco mode". By setting the priority of other applications to "low," you may free up system resources for the ones you really care about. Improved performance and battery life are expected benefits of this measure, as resource-intensive programs will no longer be able to use all of the available CPU or GPU resources.

How to find Settings in Windows 11

The Settings app in Windows 11 differs from the one in Windows 10. The Settings interface appears altered at first look. There are, of course, additional alterations. MiniTool Software will demonstrate how to access Windows 11's new Settings and how to utilize it to change your computer's settings in this post.

The Windows 11 Insider preview build claims that the operating system contains a new Settings app. The Settings app in Windows 11 may be seen in the image below. The interface is noticeably different from Windows 10.

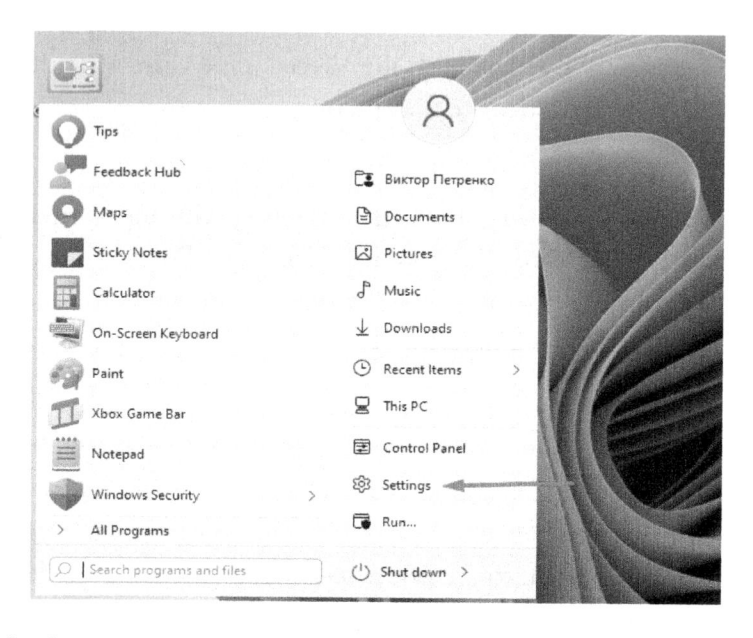

The Settings app in Windows 11 has seen some tweaks courtesy of

Microsoft. We'll now demonstrate how to access the new Windows 11 Settings and how to use it to modify your computer's settings.

How To Access Settings on Windows 11?

- Employ keyboard shortcuts
- Utilize the WinX
- Menu via the Start Menu
- the Desktop context menu
- Taskbar settings
- Notifications Settings

Using keyboard shortcuts is method one.

To activate the Settings app, simply press the Windows + I keys simultaneously.

There is still a choice in the WinX menu for Method 2: Use WinX Menu Settings. In order to activate the WinX menu, select Settings by pressing the Windows + X keys simultaneously. The WinX menu can also be accessed by right-clicking the Start button.

Third Approach: Start Menu

The Settings app is by default pinned to the Start menu in Windows 11. Utilizing the Start menu, you can access Settings.

Select Settings from the Pinned section by clicking the Start button.

Method 4: Using the desktop's context menu

To access the Settings app, right-click the desktop and choose Personalize or Display settings.

5th Approach: Using Taskbar Settings

To access the Settings page, right-click the taskbar and choose Taskbar settings.

Using the Notifications Settings is Method 6

To launch Windows 11 Settings, right-click the time and date box on the taskbar's right side and choose Notification settings.

Here are six quick ways to access Settings on Windows 11. Of course, there are a few further options. To enter the Settings program, for instance, right-click the Network and Internet or Volume icons in the taskbar and choose Sound settings or Network and Internet settings, respectively. Additionally, certain techniques for opening Settings in Windows 10 are available in Windows 11 as well.

How to Use Windows 11 New Settings?

In Windows 11 Settings, you can see the following categories:

- System
- Bluetooth & devices
- Network & internet

- Personalization
- Apps
- Accounts
- Time & language
- Gaming
- Accessibility
- Privacy & security
- Windows Update

System

System

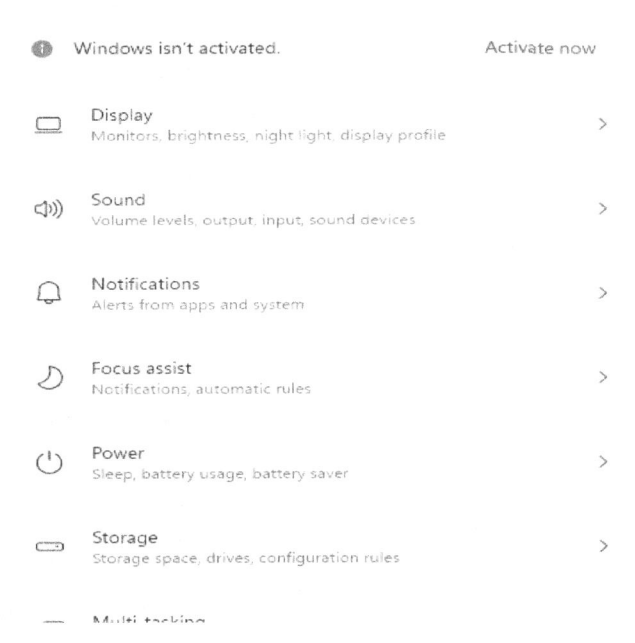

	Windows isn't activated.	Activate now
	Display Monitors, brightness, night light, display profile	>
	Sound Volume levels, output, input, sound devices	>
	Notifications Alerts from apps and system	>
	Focus assist Notifications, automatic rules	>
	Power Sleep, battery usage, battery saver	>
	Storage Storage space, drives, configuration rules	>
	Multi-tasking	

You can change the following settings for your machine under System:

1. Display\sSound\sNotifications
2. Focus support

3. Power\sStorage
4. Multitasking\sActivation
5. Desktop Clipboard Remote
6. There are some further choices.

Troubleshoot

On your computer, Troubleshoot can be used to resolve several software and hardware problems.

Recovery

System > Recovery

Fix problems without resetting your PC
Resetting can take a while — first, try resolving issues by running a troubleshooter

Recovery options

Reset this PC
Choose to keep or remove your personal files, then reinstall Windows
Reset PC

Advanced startup
Restart your device to change startup settings, including starting from a disc or USB drive
Restart now

Help with Recovery

Creating a recovery drive

Get help

You can reset your computer, go back to Windows 10 (if you upgraded to Windows 11 for more than ten days, this function won't work), go to Recovery to fix issues without restarting your computer, and modify the start-up options.

Displaying on this PC

This function allows you to mirror your Windows phone or computer onto this screen. On this page, you can also rename your machine.

You can view the characteristics of your computer and Windows in this part, as well as change several settings related to BitLocker, remote desktop, and product key and activation. In this area, you can also launch Device Manager.

Bluetooth and gadgets

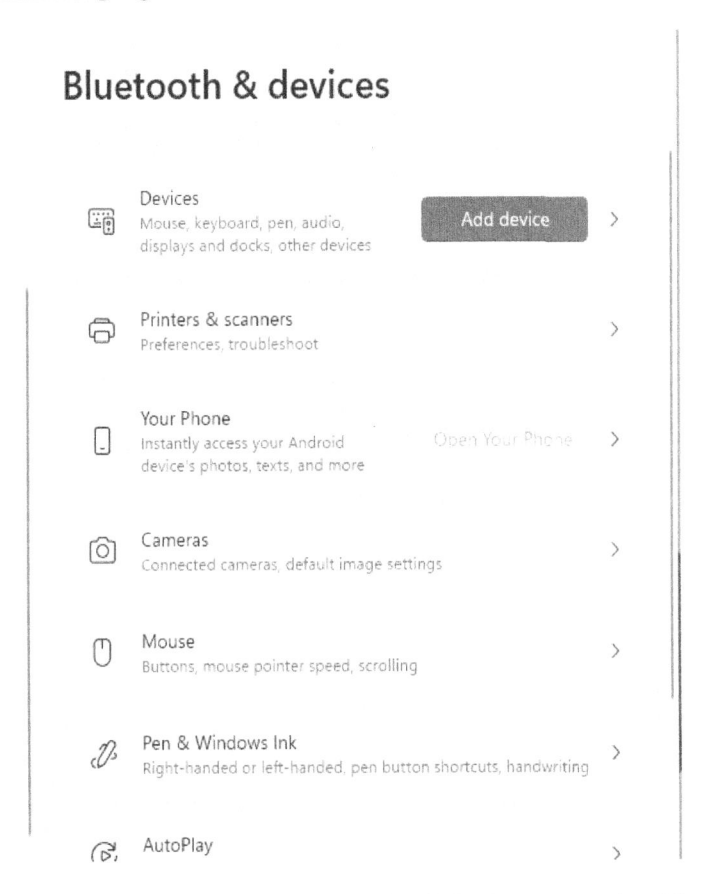

Bluetooth & devices

Devices
Mouse, keyboard, pen, audio, displays and docks, other devices   Add device   >

Printers & scanners
Preferences, troubleshoot   >

Your Phone
Instantly access your Android   Open Your Phone   >
device's photos, texts, and more

Cameras
Connected cameras, default image settings   >

Mouse
Buttons, mouse pointer speed, scrolling   >

Pen & Windows Ink
Right-handed or left-handed, pen button shortcuts, handwriting   >

AutoPlay   >

You can choose which Bluetooth-enabled device to use in this area to connect to your computer. Additionally, you can modify the settings for your USB, camera, mouse, pen & Windows Ink, and other devices.

Internet and network

You can configure your Ethernet, use a VPN, install a proxy, set up a dial-up internet connection, and use other sophisticated network settings under Network & internet.

Personalization

Personalisation

Select a theme to apply

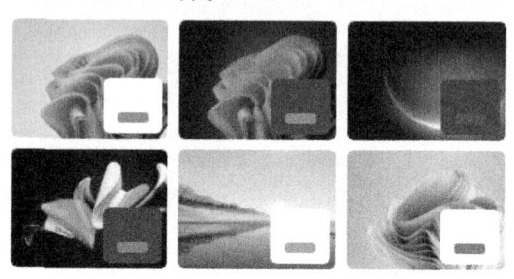

You can alter the following aspects of your computer's appearance and Personalization:

- Background\sColours
- Themes
- Screen lock Touch keyboard
- The Start button
- Taskbar\sFonts

Displaying on this PC

This function allows you to mirror your Windows phone or computer onto this screen. On this page, you can also rename your machine.

You can view the characteristics of your computer and Windows in this part, as well as change several settings related to BitLocker, remote desktop, and product key and activation. In this area, you can also launch Device Manager.

Bluetooth and gadgets

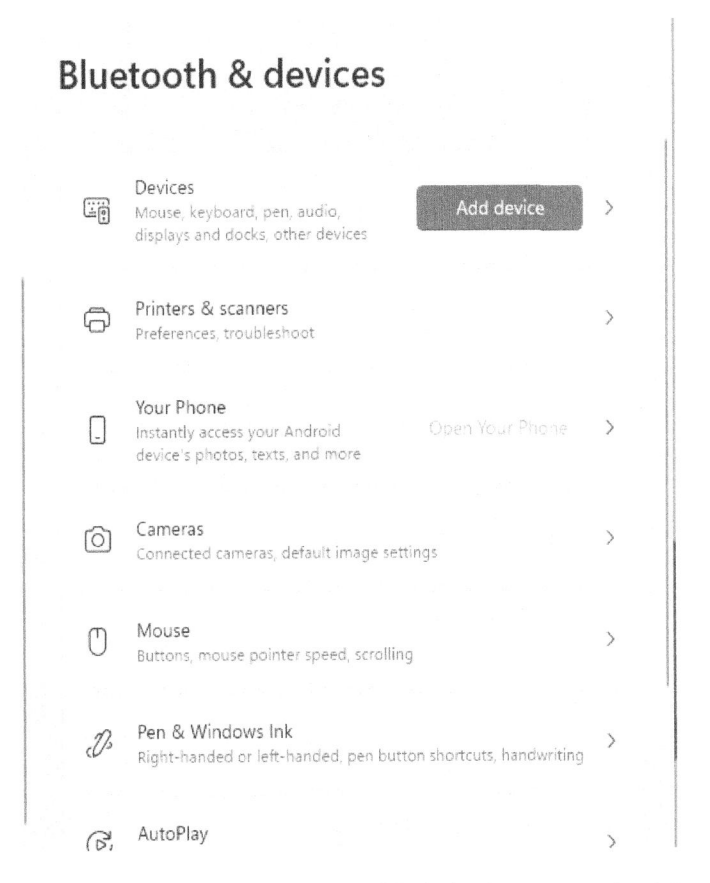

Bluetooth & devices

- Devices
  Mouse, keyboard, pen, audio, displays and docks, other devices — Add device
- Printers & scanners
  Preferences, troubleshoot
- Your Phone
  Instantly access your Android device's photos, texts, and more — Open Your Phone
- Cameras
  Connected cameras, default image settings
- Mouse
  Buttons, mouse pointer speed, scrolling
- Pen & Windows Ink
  Right-handed or left-handed, pen button shortcuts, handwriting
- AutoPlay

You can choose which Bluetooth-enabled device to use in this area to connect to your computer. Additionally, you can modify the settings for your USB, camera, mouse, pen & Windows Ink, and other devices.

Internet and network

You can configure your Ethernet, use a VPN, install a proxy, set up a dial-up internet connection, and use other sophisticated network settings under Network & internet.

Personalization

Personalisation

Select a theme to apply

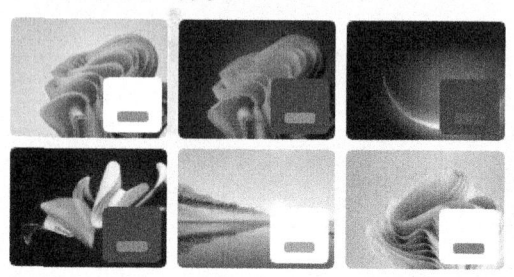

You can alter the following aspects of your computer's appearance and Personalization:

- Background\sColours
- Themes
- Screen lock Touch keyboard
- The Start button
- Taskbar\sFonts

Apps for Device Usage

You can uninstall apps from your computer, set default programs to open your files, control video playback, set startup programs, and perform other operations under the Apps heading.

Accounts

You may examine and modify your accounts' settings under Accounts. To view more information, click each choice.

Date and language

You can configure the date, time, language, area, typing patterns, and speech for your computer under Time & language.

Gaming

You can modify the settings for your Xbox Game Bar, captures, and game mode under Gaming.

Accessibility

You can modify the settings for vision, hearing, and interactivity under Accessibility.

Now you can customize and settings for your PC as you want. Make them first, and then move to the next step with this book!

Chapter 3: How to work with files and documents

Files and documents It is an important part of PC use. Who knows when you will need it? Maybe you want to save some files or create a document and write your own book, or maybe you want to see photos of your kids. Anyway, if you want to be a computer-savvy senior, you need to know this information. So, let's start

About files and folders

You have access to a wide variety of file kinds. File types include, for instance, Microsoft Word documents, digital pictures, digital music, and digital films. You might even consider a file to be a computer-interactive digital representation of a physical object. You'll frequently be reading, creating, or editing files when using several applications.

Typically, an icon is used to represent files. Below the Recycle Bin on the desktop, you may notice a few distinct kinds of files.

Describe a folder.

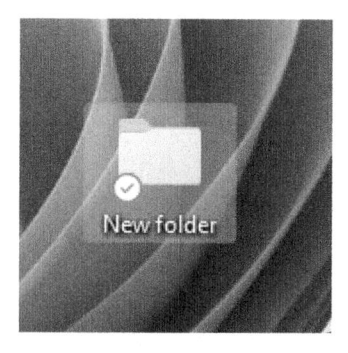

Windows employs folders to assist with file organization. Just like you would put documents within a real folder, you may place files inside of folders. You may see a desktop folder in the picture below.

Finder for files

A built-in program named File Explorer can be used to view and arrange files and directories (called Windows Explorer in Windows 7 and earlier versions).

Double-click any folder on your desktop or the File Explorer icon on the taskbar to launch File Explorer. It will open a fresh File Explorer window.

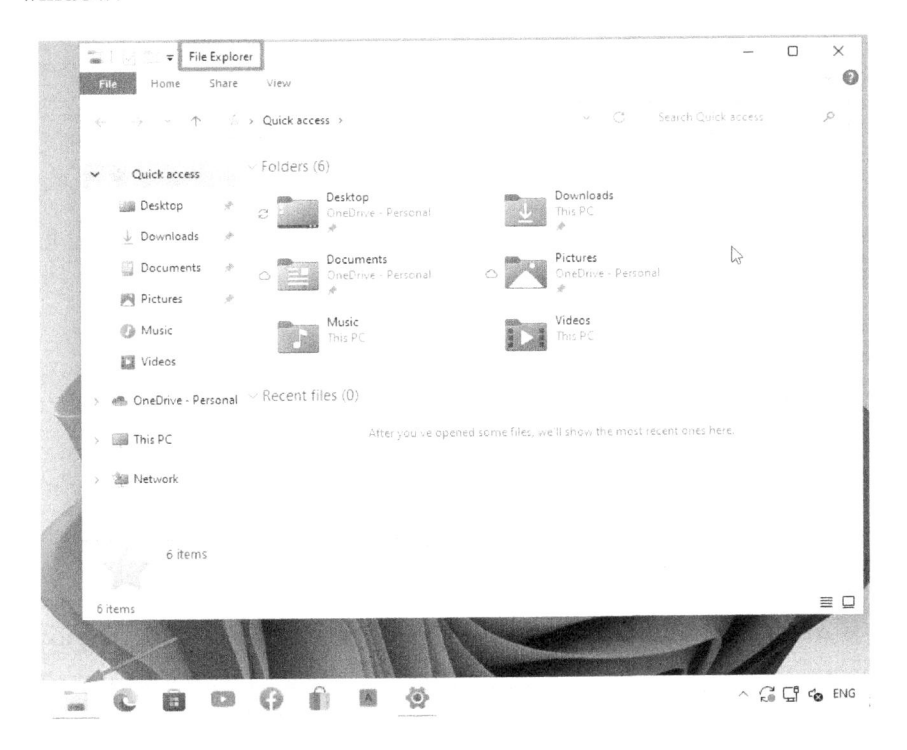

You are now prepared to interact with your files and folders.

Double-clicking a folder in File Explorer will open it. All of the files kept in that folder are then visible to you.

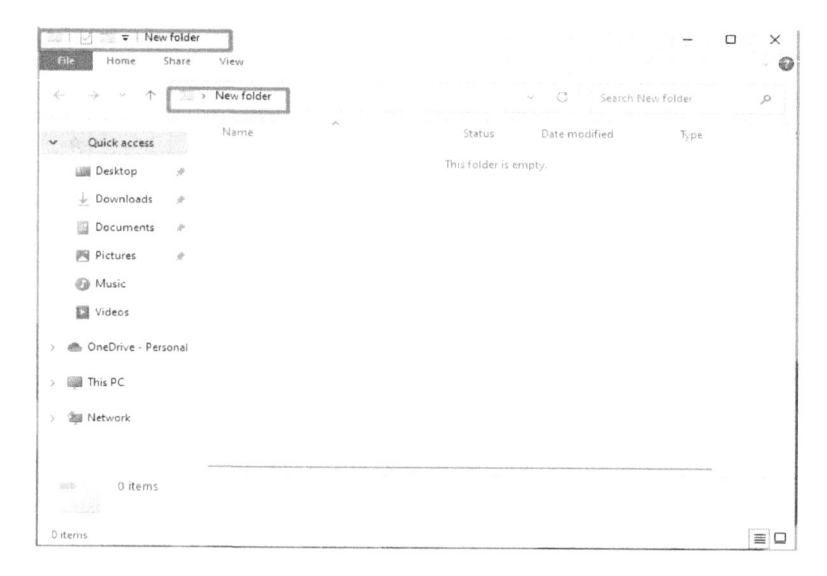

Observe that the address bar at the top of the window lets you know where a folder is located as well.

Open a file by:

Opening a file can be done in one of two ways:

Double-click the file after locating it on your PC. By doing this, the file will open in its default application.

Launch the application, then use it to access the file. When the program is running, you can choose Open from the File menu at the top of the window.

File relocating and deletion

As you start utilizing your computer, you'll begin to accumulate an increasing number of files, which can make it more challenging to locate the information you require. Thankfully, Windows lets you transfer files across directories and remove files that are no longer needed.

Moving a file is simple; you can do it from one place to another. For instance, you could want to move a file from your desktop to your Documents folder.

Drag the file with a click to the desired area

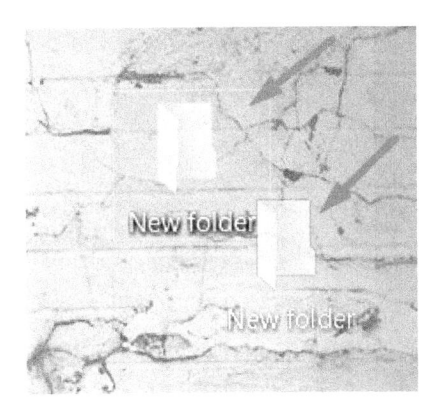

Let go of the mouse. In the new place, the file will show up.

The same method can be used to relocate a whole folder. It should be noted that relocating a folder also moves all of the files contained within it.

To make a new folder, locate and click the New folder button in File Explorer. The folder can also be created by right-clicking the desired location and choosing New > Folder.

There will be a brand-new folder. Press Enter after entering the folder's desired name. We'll call it School Documents in our example.

There will be a new folder made. Moving files into this folder is now possible.

Change the name of any file or folder by clicking on the appropriate button. It will be simpler to recall what kind of information is stored in the file or folder if it has a distinctive name.

After roughly a second, click the file or folder again. You'll see a text field you can change.

On the keyboard, type the desired name and hit Enter. There will be a name change.

Rename can also be chosen from the pop-up menu by right-clicking the folder

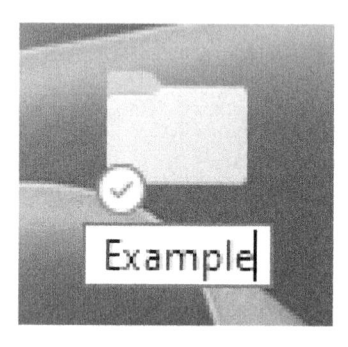

To delete a file or folder: You can delete a file that you no longer need. A file is relocated to the Recycle Bin when it is deleted. You can return the file from the Recycle Bin to its original location if you change your mind. You must empty the Recycle Bin if you are certain you want to permanently delete the file.

The file should be clicked and then dragged to the desktop's Recycle Bin icon. To pick a file, click on it, and then press the Delete key on your keyboard.

Right-click the Recycle Bin icon and choose Empty Recycle Bin to permanently delete the file. The Recycle Bin will permanently erase all files.

Keep in mind that when you delete a folder, you also delete all of the files contained within it.

Choosing numerous files

After learning the fundamentals, consider the following advice to move your files even more quickly.

Choosing several files

There are a few techniques for selecting several files simultaneously:

You can click and drag the mouse to create a box around the files you want to pick when seeing your files as icons. Release the mouse button when finished, and the files will be selected. All of these files can now be moved, copied, or deleted at the same time.

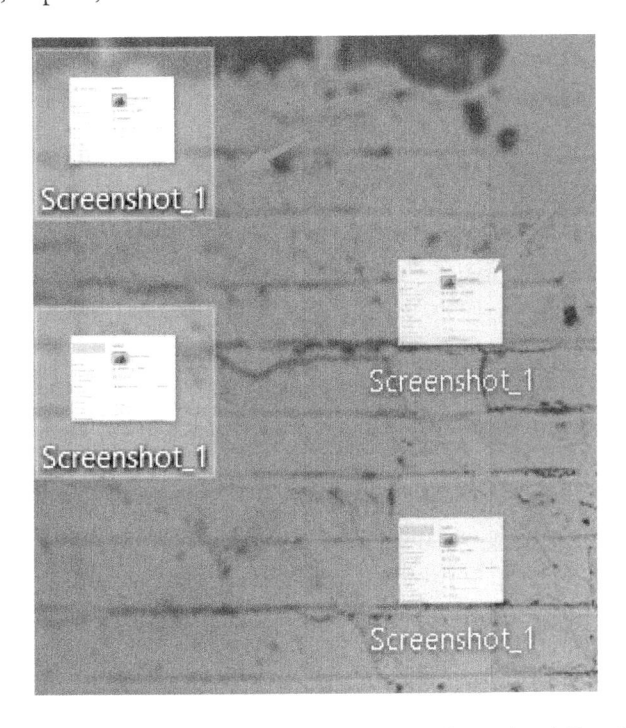

Press and hold the Control key on your keyboard while clicking the desired files to select them from a folder.

Click the first file in a folder, hold down the Shift key on your keyboard, and then click the last file to select all of those files. The first file and the last file will both be chosen.

Choosing all files

Open the folder in File Explorer and click Ctrl+A to pick every file in the folder at once (press and hold the Control key on your keyboard, then press A). The entire contents of the folder will be chosen.

Don't worry if managing files and folders right now seems a little challenging. Working with files and folders is mostly a matter of practice, like anything else. As you use your computer more, you'll start to feel more at ease.

Shortcuts

Making a shortcut on your desktop for a file or folder you use frequently will save you time.

You can access a shortcut by double-clicking it rather than having to navigate to the file or folder each time you need to utilize it.

The icon for a shortcut will include a little arrow in the bottom-left corner.

It should be noted that establishing a shortcut just makes it easier to reach a folder; it does not duplicate the folder itself.

The real folder or the files inside it will not be deleted if you delete a shortcut. Also keep in mind that transferring a shortcut to a file onto a flash drive will not work; instead, if you wish to bring a file with you, you must travel to the file's actual location and copy it.

Locate the appropriate folder, then right-click it and choose Send to Desktop to create a shortcut (create shortcut).

On the desktop, a shortcut to the folder will show up. Take note of the arrow in the icon's lower-left corner.

Now, double-click the shortcut to always open the folder.

To create a shortcut, click the folder, hold down the Alt key on your computer, and then drag it to the desktop.

You can make the same action with any type of files: images, video, audio, documents. Now let's talk about documents.

Microsoft Word

If you're unfamiliar with Microsoft Word, don't panic; it's never too late to master this essential application. In little time at all, you will have mastered the fundamentals and be able to use this popular tool efficiently. This tutorial will assist you with the essentials.

What is Microsoft Word and what purpose does it serve?

Microsoft Word is one of the most popular word processing applications currently available. Word processing is the computer-based generation of text. Microsoft Word is used to generate digital documents for personal and professional purposes. It is capable of several functions, all of which are aimed at enhancing the text-writing experience.

Microsoft Word is used to write letters, lesson plans, articles, novels, edit documents, construct resumes, and create newsletters. It occasionally serves as a placeholder for unpublished papers, allowing users to add information before making the document public. It also guarantees the correctness of the creation's spelling and grammar.

Microsoft Word enables users to produce digital letters and other documents.

How to create a new document and save it

If you would prefer to create a document from scratch, launch Microsoft Word. The 'Home' tab of the application will display, allowing you to choose a template type. Click the "blank document" symbol if you're searching for a clean slate on which to write. Find the appropriate template for additional tasks, such as producing a resume or professional letter (there is a "more templates" option beneath the icons if the one you want isn't displayed).

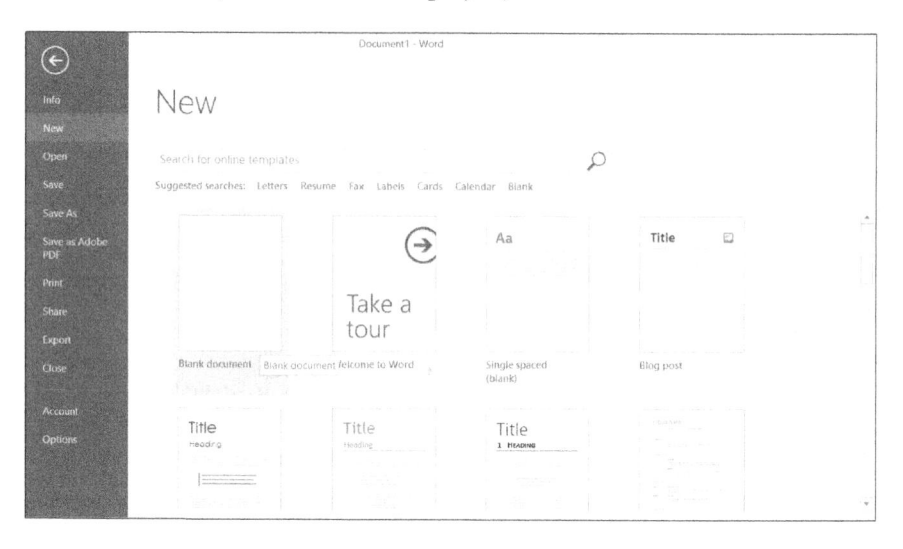

Once you have written your document, you should frequently save it to prevent inadvertent deletion or file loss due to hardware failure. Using auto-save is one way to prevent this from occurring. Select 'AutoSave' in the top left corner by toggling the blue checkbox to 'On'. Note that this needs the use of OneDrive, Microsoft's cloud service (OneDrive for business is also available). If you do not utilize autosave, take care to save your project periodically while writing. Click the blue disk symbol in the upper left corner to save your file. A pop-up box will appear if this is the first time you've saved this document, requesting you to name the file and select a place on your computer. Next, let's ensure that you understand how to adjust certain text settings.

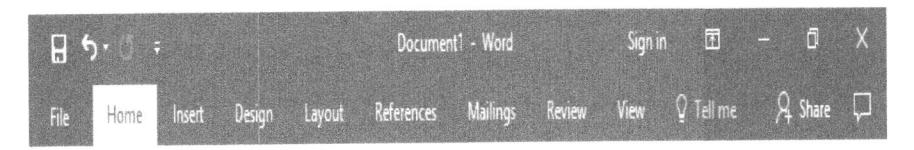

Click the button labeled "Blank document" to begin with a blank page.

How to modify the format and dimensions of your document

Text layouts and sizes that appeal to various individuals vary based on the sort of document being created. The standard font size for every blank document is Calibri (font) 11. (font size). If these parameters are suitable for your project, there is no reason to modify them. However, here's how to increase/decrease the size and/or alter the look of text.

Determine first whether you like the font style. If you don't like it, look for the toolbar at the top of the page. It should be in the 'Home' tab by default.

If not, select the "Home" option. Next, locate the drop-down option that includes font styles ('Calibri' should be the default). Click it and select the desired style from the list of alternatives. Note that if you alter the font, the size of the text may increase, as certain styles are larger than others. Consider this while picking your font size. Find the dropdown menu next to the font style to modify the font size. The appropriate size would be 11. Click it and choose the number/size that best fits you. Now that the sizes and styles have been determined, it is time to import external images and construct tables.

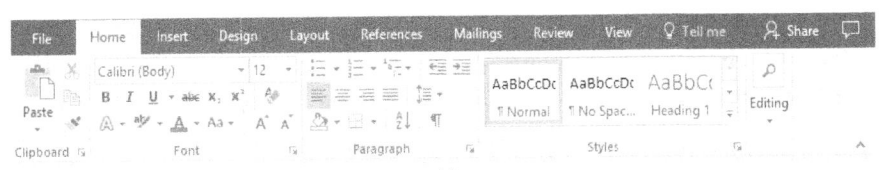

Using a dropdown menu, the font style may be altered.

How to incorporate tables, page numbers, and images

Microsoft Word enables users to include a vast array of functionalities into a document. These are especially beneficial for tasks requiring diverse statistical and data presentations. Start the table creation process by clicking the "Insert" tab. Choose the 'Table' icon from this tab. A drop-down menu will be displayed. Click and choose the desired number of rows and columns for your table from this menu.

Images and page numbers may be inserted using the same 'Insert' tab. Choose the 'Pictures' icon and go to the relevant file on your computer using the pop-up box. To add a page number, click the 'Page Number' icon and pick the location in the selection menu that appears. Now that you understand how to perform the bare minimum using Word, here are a few key techniques to accelerate your learning.

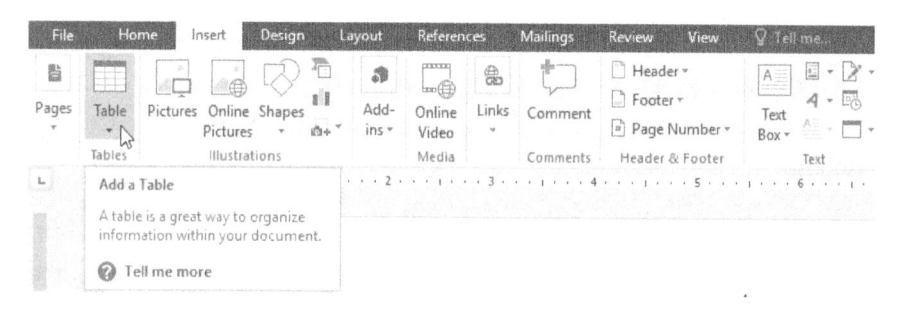

The 'Table' icon provides many table insertion choices.

Some fundamental advice to aid you in your endeavors

These suggestions won't teach you all there is to know about Word, but they will make your life much simpler.

How to do an internal document search

To search your document for certain words or numbers, hold the 'CTRL' key and hit the 'F' key simultaneously. A window will popup, allowing you to enter any desired sentence.

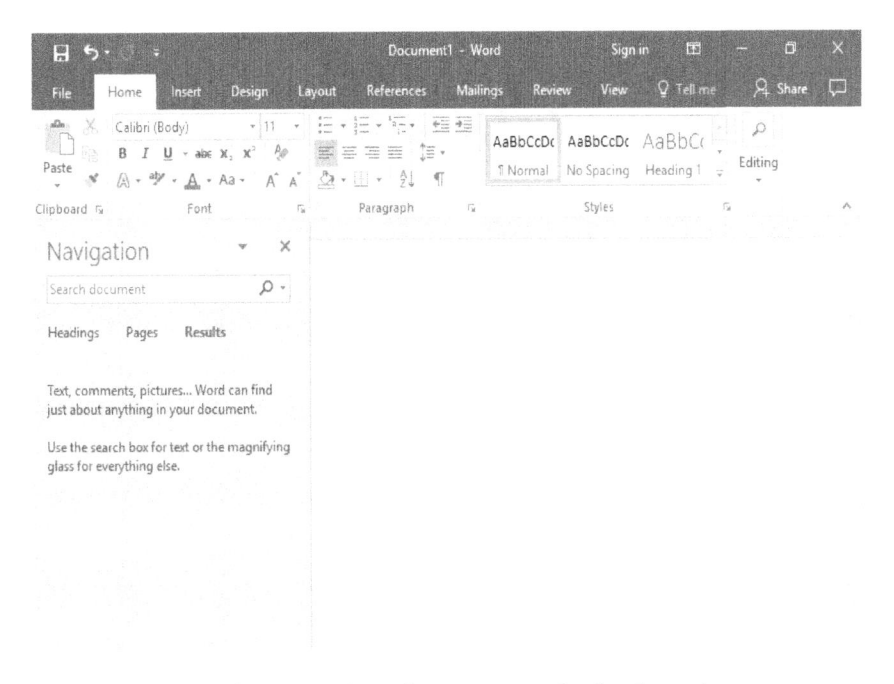

How to copy and paste using shortcuts on the keyboard

It is possible to copy and paste using the menu, but it will take significantly longer. A handful of times may not seem like a huge problem, but it mounts up over a lifetime of Word use. To copy anything, use the mouse to select it, hold down the 'CTRL' key, and then press the 'C' key. Then, move to the desired location, hold down the 'CTRL' key, and hit the 'V' key. Even if you're just beginning to learn how to use Microsoft Word, there's no reason you can't be successful. Follow the fundamental advice and features outlined in this tutorial, and you will be successful.

Chapter 4: About the Internet

The internet provides a wealth of opportunities for keeping in touch with loved ones, learning useful information, and even shopping and paying bills from the convenience of your home. If you've never used the internet before, it could seem intimidating, but as you start taking baby steps, you'll realize it's a lot more approachable than you might think.

You must, of course, take steps in order to protect your data online. However, some of the scary tales you may have heard exaggerate the dangers of using the internet. In this chapter, we'll look at ways to keep you secure and recommend some additional reading if you want to learn more. We will also look at technical jargon, which could be confusing at first but makes sense after you become familiar with it.

Finally, we'll examine some of the numerous advantages that the internet can bring to your life, regardless of your age. The internet's core purpose is to facilitate communication and closer human connections. Whether it's your grandchild on a gap year of travel or the neighborhood department shop where you want to buy a new vacuum.

Make a cup of tea, read this guide thoroughly, and then go through it section by section as you put some of the suggestions into practice and explore the great world of the internet.

Seniors' Access to the Internet and Technical Jargon

If you don't want to begin using a computer at home right away, your local library should have PCs where you may practice basic computer skills. They might even offer beginner's internet lessons. This may be a good place to begin. Let's look at what you'll need if you're prepared to connect to the internet from your house.

A laptop

Typically, a PC with Microsoft Windows loaded will do. In either case, you'll need to use a program known as a browser to access the internet.

There are a number of browser choices available if you buy a Windows-based PC, including Chrome, Firefox, and Microsoft Edge.

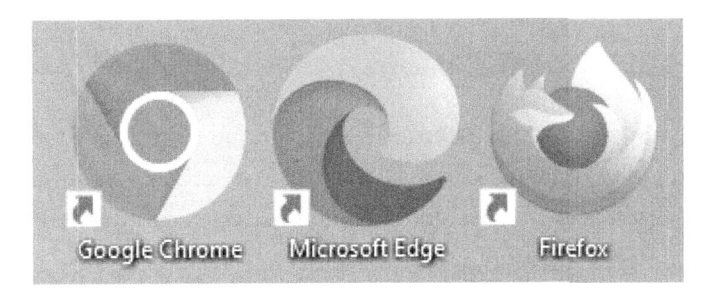

Your computer might be a desktop model with a separate tower, monitor screen, keyboard, and mouse as one last difference. It might also be a laptop with all the features you require built in. The latter gives you more freedom in where you employ it.

Internet connection

There are numerous businesses that can give you broadband internet access. ISPs, or Internet Service Providers, are the names of these businesses. Broadband speeds can differ depending on where you live geographically and the ISP you choose. Depending on how much data you need and how much you want to pay each month, this Which guide will help you choose the broadband package that is ideal for you.

The Router

You will receive a router from your chosen ISP once you have contracted with them and made your choice. Basically, this is a tiny gadget that connects your computer to the internet and allows data to travel both ways. A router may support Wi-Fi connectivity in addition to cable connections. Wi-Fi uses radio waves, much like your mobile phone, to connect to the internet without the use of cables. Wi-Fi has the benefit of enabling you to use a laptop or tablet from anywhere in the house.

You may now sit down in front of your computer, equipped with everything you need to access the internet, and get started exploring. You'll want to navigate the internet once your preferred browser has been opened. Let's look at how.

What Does a Web Address Mean?

Every website on the internet has a unique address, which you may enter into the browser bar at the top of the screen if you know it. Let's look at a well-known website URL and analyze each element.

The 'http' or 'https' protocol comes first. What distinguishes these two from one another?

When utilizing websites relating to anything financial, such as online banking or when entering your credit card information to make a purchase, you should always check that the "s" stands for secure.

It is an additional layer of security that the merchant employs to prevent unauthorized parties from accessing your data.

The next letter, "www," stands for "world wide web," another name for the internet. We can access information from all over the world thanks to the "world wide web," which is a network of networks connected on a global scale.

The name of the website itself, which is frequently a brand name like Facebook, comes next. This address's final "com" is referred to as an extension. The extension indicates if the address belongs to a business, an organization, a school, or even a nation. This tutorial includes examples of several different extensions as well as explanations of what each one means.

Seniors' Guide to Search Engines

When using Facebook as an example, we can fill in the website address if we know it. What happens if you don't have an address but are looking for information instead, like the name of a nearby plumber, a video lesson on how to make a skirt, or the time the post office opens on Tuesday?

The good news is that you only need a "search engine" to locate all of this information, which puts it right at your fingers. Given that the term "biggest search engine" has now become commonplace, I'm confident you've heard of it. Google is the in question search engine. Although there are other choices, such as Bing and Yahoo, which you should test out to determine which works best for you, Google will be the one we'll be using throughout this guide.

A search box with the Google logo above it will display in the middle of your screen as soon as you put Google into the web address bar at the top of your browser. Then, you can type in anything you're looking for.

Gmail   Images

Google

Google Search   I'm Feeling Lucky

A lengthy list of search results that may span many pages will subsequently be presented to you. If you want to see all of them, you must scroll all the way down and select the "next page" link at the bottom of the screen. The results that Google's search engine thinks are the most relevant to your search, however, will be displayed at the top of the first page. Click around on the websites it suggests here for a while until you locate what you're looking for. If you don't discover exactly what you're looking for, you might be able to improve your search results by gently altering your query.

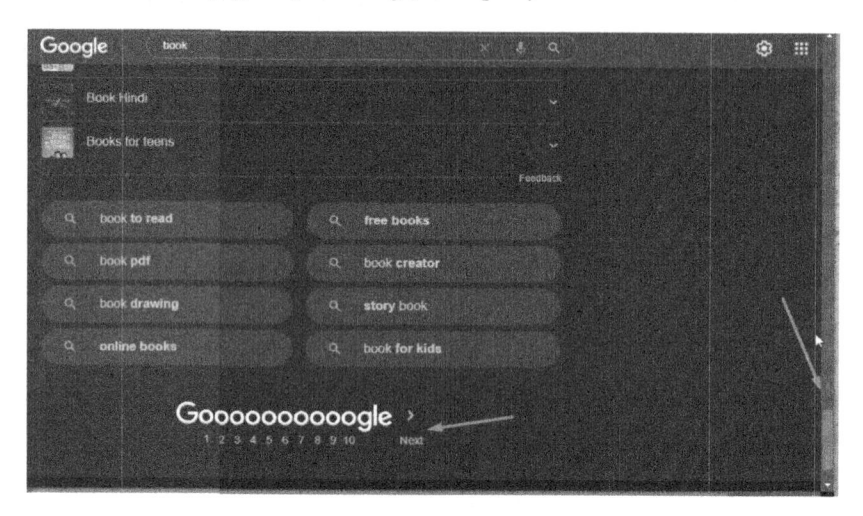

Blogs and social networks

Social media and blogs are two aspects of the internet that are worth mentioning since they make it easy to stay in touch with existing friends and family as well as establish new ones. Social media platforms include websites like Facebook, Twitter, YouTube, Pinterest, and Instagram, and they serve as venues for communication, conversation, and information sharing.

In addition to live chatting and watching short videos, members of the social networking site Facebook may also leave comments, upload photos, exchange links to news articles and other relevant online information, and more.

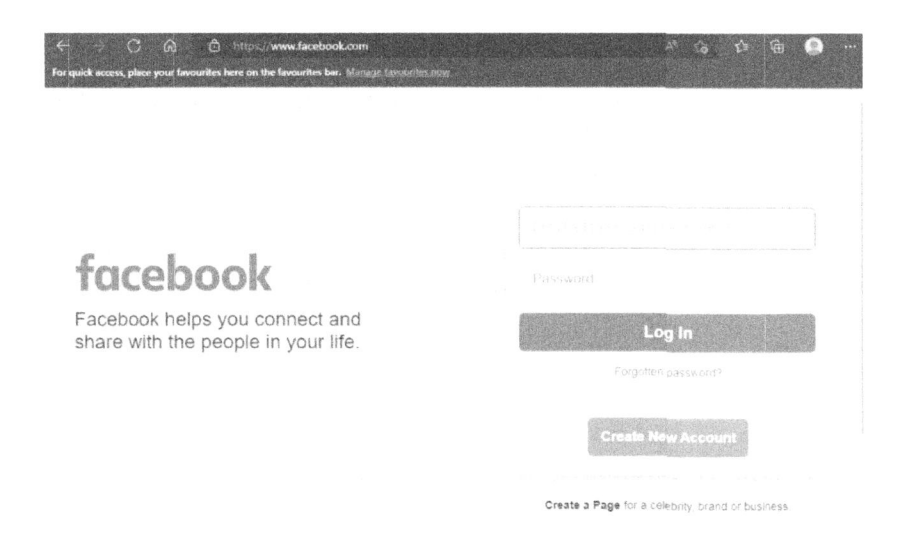

YouTube is a popular video-sharing platform. Millions of people all around the world have signed up for the service so they may share their movies with the world. More than 35 hours of video are added to YouTube each and every minute of the day.

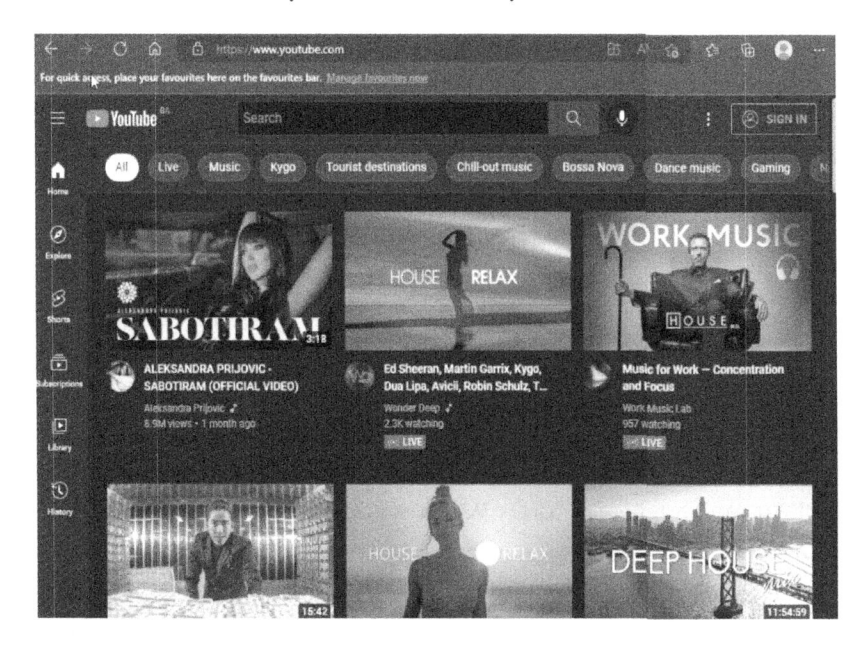

Social media is a good location to learn more about local and international companies if you're thinking about doing business with them because both people and businesses may be found there.

A blog is a website that people or businesses routinely update with new content, known as posts (the shorter form of the broader word weblog). Blogs might be in the form of an online diary or they can be about nearly any topic, including crafts or classic vehicle collecting.

Keeping Seniors Safe Online

We've already proven that you can access a vast amount of information on the internet, but how can you keep secure while doing so?

Let's look at the principal techniques for enhancing browsing security:

<u>Install antivirus software first.</u>

On the internet, there are dangerous individuals whose sole goal is to infect computers with malware. Malware is software that tries to interfere with your computer's operation, steal your personal information, or even prevent your computer from functioning altogether. You should regularly scan your computer for harmful software because malware is constantly changing. Installing and maintaining updated antivirus software is the best way to accomplish this. Whatever program you decide on, you can easily arrange it to automatically update and check your computer every day for any problems. In the event that malware is discovered during the scan, it will be quarantined and removed before it can cause any issues.

If you're running Windows 11, you already have a free antivirus application built-in Windows Defender. Microsoft Windows has this built-in anti-malware tool. Windows Defender doesn't need to be supplemented with any extra anti-virus software in order to do its job. The Windows Defender antivirus software is also known as Windows Security, Microsoft Defender, Windows Antivirus, and Microsoft

Antivirus.

You can find it in this menu:

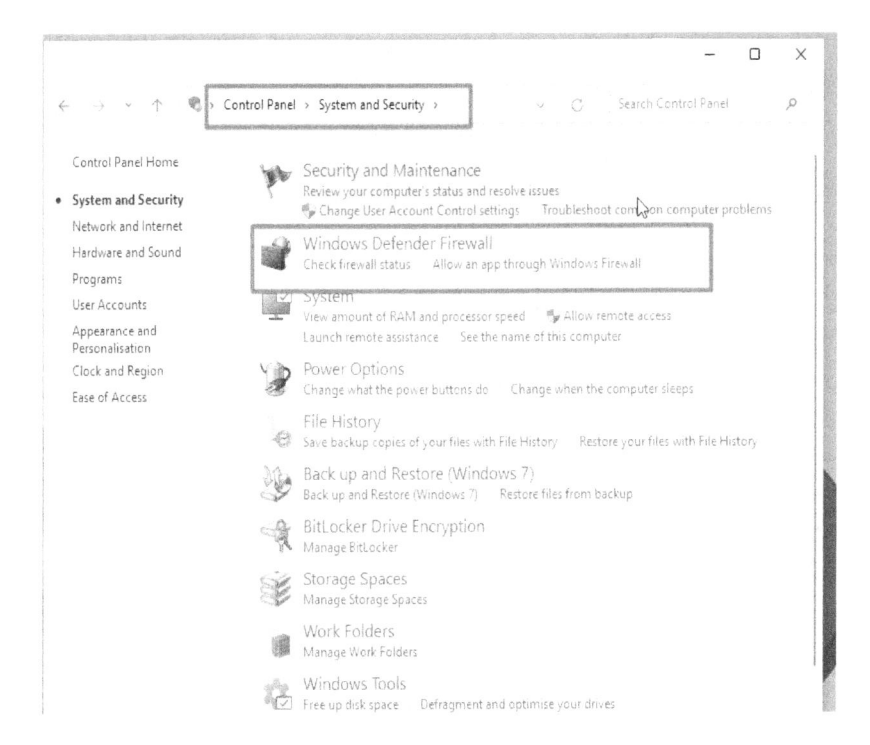

Selecting Strong Passwords

Always choose lengthy passwords for your online accounts that contain a combination of upper- and lowercase letters, digits, and special characters. Pick unique passwords for every account you have, and never share your password with anyone. In order to prevent outsiders from accessing your data, make sure any Wi-Fi networks you have at home are password-protected.

Watch out for phishing

When you get an email from what appears to be a trustworthy source, like your bank or a retailer, asking you to click on a link or enter personal information, that email is phishing. These emails, however, are frauds that attempt to commit fraud and are not from the person or company they claim to be. Always be suspicious of any email you receive because some of these may seem real. Contact the organization directly by phone if you wish to confirm that the correspondence came from them. The same is true if you get an email attachment from an unknown sender. Never open the attachment since it can be infected with malware.

Seniors' Online Banking

Life may be made a lot simpler by online banking. You can avoid standing in line at your neighborhood branch and make transfers of money to and from your account as well as round-the-clock bill payments.

The aforementioned advice should all be put into practice prior to conducting any online banking because it will help keep you safe. Additionally, you can ask your bank if they have two-step authentication, which will make you even safer. For instance, you might be able to set up your online banking such that each time you log in, a different code is sent to you through text message. This guarantees that you are the one accessing your account and not a fraudster.

Never divulge your user name or password to anyone over the phone or in an email, even if they claim to be from the bank. In any case, a bank will never request this information. Always review your bank statements as an extra precaution, and if you discover a transaction you don't recognize, report it to the bank right away.

Online purchasing

The majority of trustworthy online retailers will go to great lengths to persuade you that shopping with them is secure. However, before you make a purchase, make sure the following are in place to guarantee you are as secure as possible.

Secure Web Address: Earlier, we discussed the need for online stores to begin their web addresses with https rather than http. Always verify that this is the case on the website before entering your personal or credit card information.

Physical Address: If you shop at a store whose name you are familiar with, especially if they have a high street presence, this can give you a certain sense of assurance. A genuine physical location and phone number should be provided if the website belongs to a less well-known retailer.

Terms & Conditions: Review the privacy statement of the retailer to learn what they will and won't do with your personal information. There should be a guarantee that they won't pass them around or sell them to anyone else. Additionally, always make sure you review the store's return and cancellation policies.

One last recommendation for online banking and shopping is to only use your own computer or a computer you are confident is secure. It is better to avoid taking the chance of making a purchase or using a public computer to access your bank account. Additionally, avoid using your laptop, tablet, or mobile device to access your bank account or make purchases on unprotected Wi-Fi networks like those found in bars and coffee shops.

Utilizing the Internet to its Fullest

We've discussed keeping yourself safe online as well as two major benefits of the internet: shopping and banking. It's time to focus on other ways we can utilize the internet to its full potential.

Establish an Email Account

If you plan to do nearly anything online, you'll need an email address because that's how you'll get login information and confirmations that accounts have been created for you. Additionally, e-mail makes it simpler and quicker to stay in touch with friends and family, particularly if they are dispersed throughout the nation or even the globe. Use a free email service like Gmail, Yahoo Mail, or Hotmail. A different option is to set up an email account with your ISP, which is frequently accessible through Microsoft Outlook.

Social media

We stated how social media is a terrific way to stay in touch with family, but it's also a great opportunity to reconnect with long-lost acquaintances or meet new people who share your interests. Just as a side note, if you ever choose to meet with someone you have only spoken to online, make sure to do so in a public setting and preferably bring a friend or family member. Let someone know where you're going, at the very least. People online may not always be what they seem to be, and they may conceal themselves behind a phony profile. Despite the fact that you don't need to worry excessively about it, it's always a good idea to be cautious at any age.

Research

The internet is a terrific resource for research on everything you're interested in, from genealogy to auto repair. If you want to acquire a new pastime or are having trouble mastering a skill, YouTube.com has a wide selection of lesson videos on subjects ranging from crochet to astrophysics.

If you're trying to plan a trip, either domestically or internationally, the internet is a great resource for information. You can organize your itinerary for a trip, search at rail schedules, and get thorough driving directions. One of the benefits of the internet is that it actually has something to fascinate everyone.

Resources and Websites

As we progressed through this tutorial, a few helpful resources were already mentioned, but here are a few more that you might find beneficial as you learn more about what the internet has to offer.

Webwise by BBC

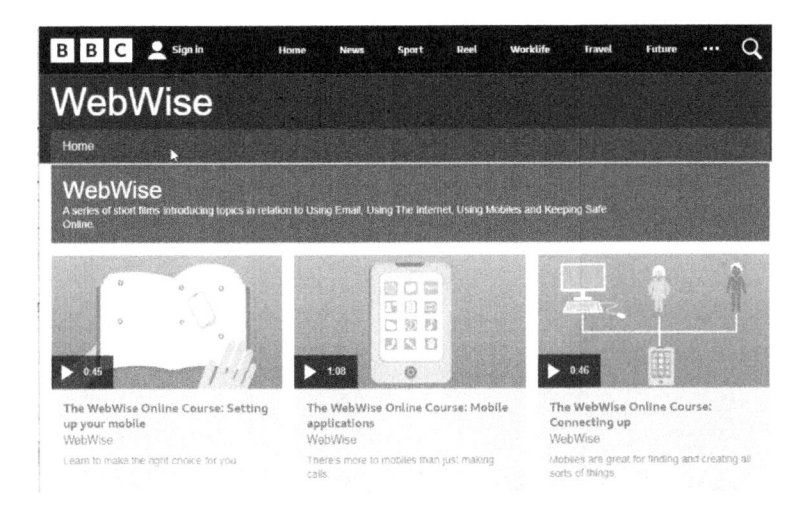

This website provides a plethora of knowledge about enhancing your digital literacy and discovering what the internet has to offer. Once you're online, it's a terrific place to begin.

Wikipedia

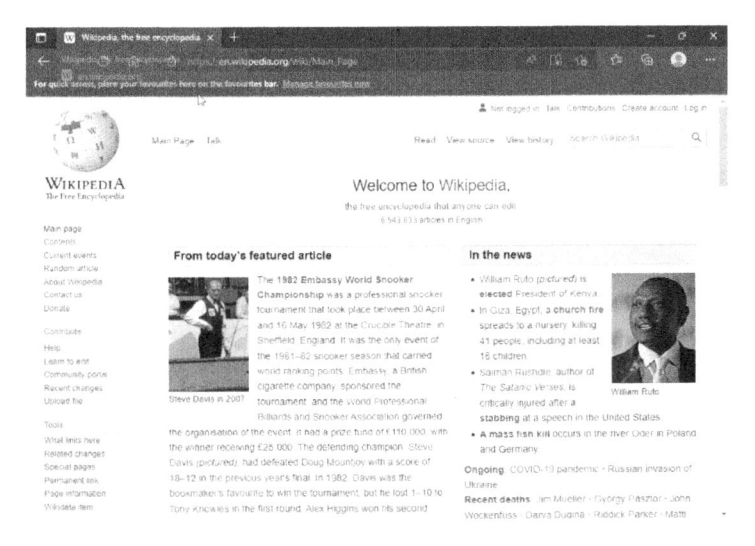

Wikipedia is a free online encyclopedia that provides details on practically any topic you can imagine. It's a good place to start any research journey.

Internet markets

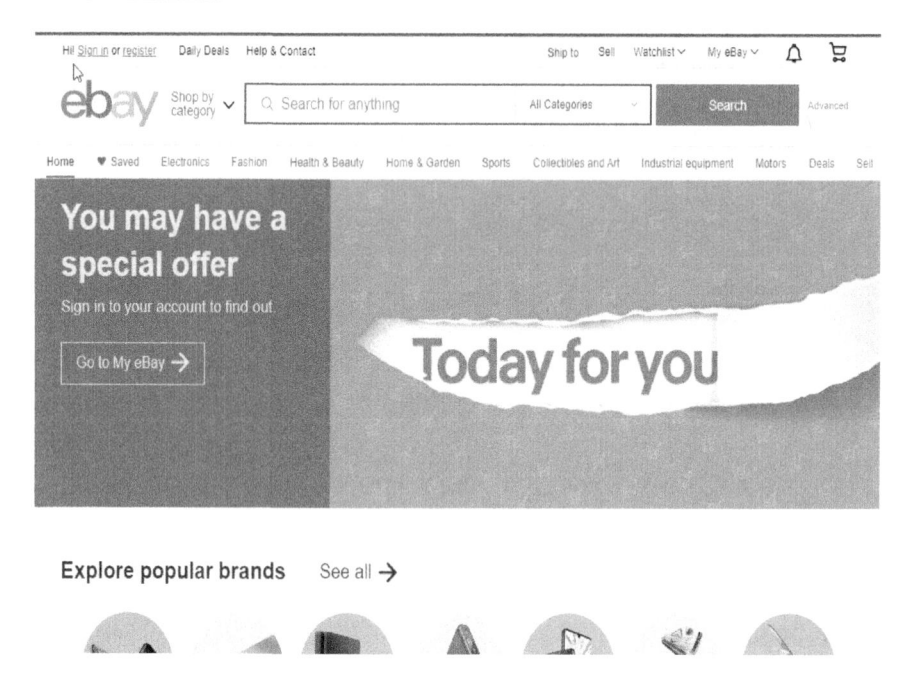

There are a ton of independent stores, but there are also marketplaces that house a large number of sellers. One of the most well-known is eBay, but there are also websites like Etsy.com and Folksy.com if you're interested in handcrafted goods.

Health

If you experience any health issues a decent place to start for any non-emergency issues is the NHS website. You can examine your symptoms, discover your condition's diagnosis, and get encouragement for pursuing therapy.

Chapter 5: Communication with family and Friends

The central component of any information system is the computer, which plays a vital role in all forms of modern communication. Household Internet use took up in the early 1990s, paving the way for the proliferation of online communication tools like email, websites, blogs, social networking, video chat, and Voice over Internet Protocol. Postal mail and landline telephones are two examples of once-common but now mostly irrelevant forms of communication.

Web and Electronic Mail

The development of the World Wide Web, the Internet, and electronic mail significantly altered the way people interact with one another. We no longer need to wait days or weeks to get data; instead, we can now see everything at the speed of light. Because of its convenience and speed, email has revolutionized the way in which people communicate and do business. Since computers can handle data at a rate of about 20 million bytes per second, they can quickly and easily download and display almost any text email.

Voice over Internet Protocol with Real-Time Video Communication

VOIP, or Voice Over Internet Protocol, has mostly supplanted traditional landline telephones. These lines are generally less expensive than traditional landlines and allow for instantaneous phone connection through the Internet. Video chats are also a feature of these communications channels, allowing you to view the other person while you talk to them. VOIP apps also save your contacts in case you need to quickly reach someone. As of May 2011, one of the biggest drawbacks of VOIP is that it makes it impossible for 911 operators to track a call's origin.

Online Social Interactions

Facebook, Twitter, and LinkedIn are just a few examples of popular social networking sites where users can easily create and share information with their networks in a short amount of time. Instead of exchanging one-off messages, social networks enable a continuous flow of updates and information. These digital technologies have advanced communication past email by enabling users to instantaneously share life and status updates with a wide audience, who in turn may react to and discuss the updates in real time. While email's distribution lists make it easy to share the same message with a wide audience, the simplified and intuitive nature of social networking sites prevents the information overload that would result from trying to do the same things via email.

Routing

Routers, while not PCs per se, are special computers designed to manage data transmissions. They are vital to the appropriate routing of communications across the Internet. Routers are devices that take "packets" of data and forward them to the correct destination. They can be utilized in the comfort of one's own home, or in one of several centralized data warehouses where all traffic is directed.

In the next paragraphs I will tell you about the most popular services for communication. I hope they will help you to keep in touch with friends and family.

Gmail

If you are one of the 1.5 billion people who use Gmail, you are not alone. Gmail has a spam filtering mechanism already installed, and it gives you 15GB of free space to store your messages.

It also has a number of time-saving features, such as the ability to schedule emails in advance, sync your calendar with your contacts, and tailor your dashboard to your specific needs. Some of its more salient characteristics are outlined below.

1. **Signing Up Setting up a new free Gmail account** is simple. A first name, last name, email address (ending in @gmail.com by default), and a password are all that are required. Setting up a Google Workspace (previously G-Suite) account (which costs as little as $5 per month) is required if you want to establish a business, nonprofit, or school.

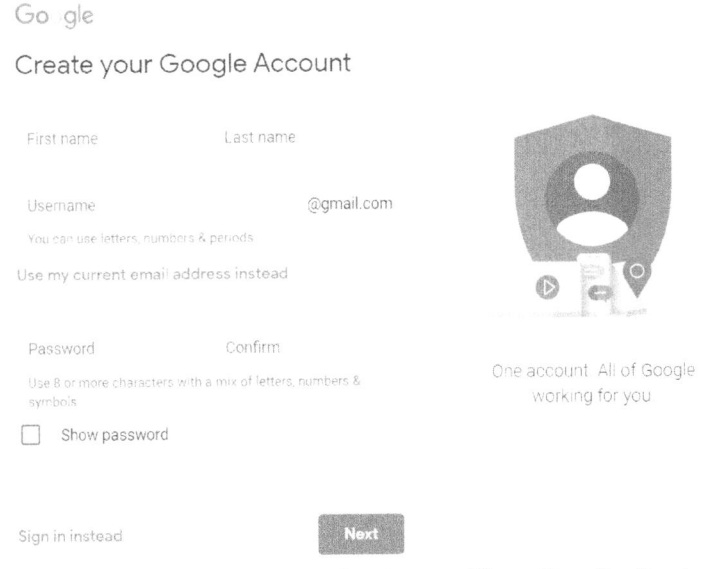

2. **Gmail's Configuration Options**. The Gmail Settings page provides access to a broad range of customization choices, including those for the inbox's appearance and security settings, as well as those for forwarding emails and other useful tools.

3. **Quick Settings** also provide options to customize your inbox by adjusting the Density, Theme, Inbox Type, and Reading pane location.

4. **Sending an Electronic Message.** To start a new email on Gmail, simply click the box labeled "Compose." Next, compose your email's body before sending it off by filling out the To, CC/BCC, and Subject areas. Spelling and grammatical errors are flagged as you type to encourage you to proofread your message before submitting it. If you highlight some text and then click the link button, the highlighted text will become a clickable hyperlink.

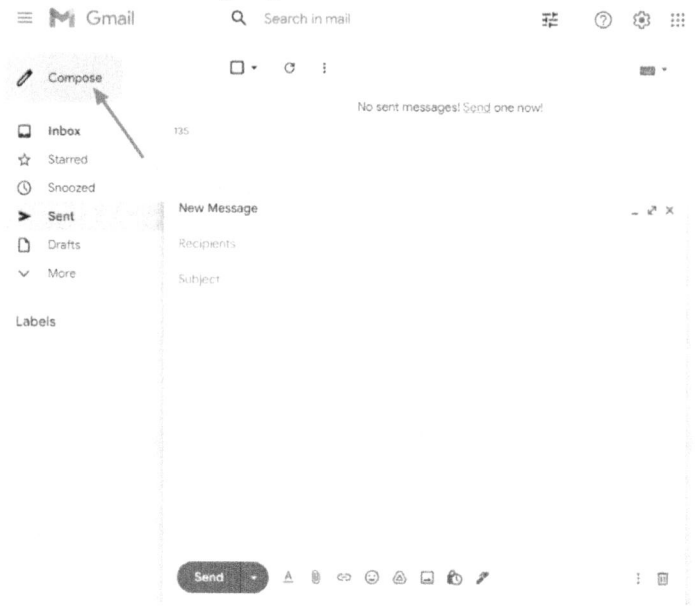

Attachments may be added by selecting the paperclip symbol and selecting the file to upload from your computer (alternatively, you can drag and drop the file). You may also attach photographs by selecting them from your computer and then clicking the "photos" icon in the email's footer.

5. **Getting Your Email in Order. Gmail's customizable interface** allows you to better manage your inbox and get more

done each day. There are a number of ways to organize your inbox to best meet your needs, including folders, labels, tabs, stars, and formatted inboxes.

6. **Labels, Tabs, and Folders.** Your inbox, drafts, sent, and trash folders are all examples of Folders in Gmail. The content of these cannot be altered in any way. However, Labels —although comparable to folders – don't operate in precisely the same manner. When an email thread or discussion thread defies categorization, for instance, you can apply the same label to many instances. Labels in Gmail provide you far more choice over how you arrange and locate your emails and chats within your inbox. There are three default email columns that appear as tabs: Primary, Social, and Promotions. You may also modify your settings to deactivate them and/or activate other panels (choosing from Updates and Forums).

7. **Processing Your Emails in Order of Importance.** Your Gmail inbox will always sort new messages in reverse chronological order, with the most recent ones showing up first. However, if it fits you better to see your most essential emails first, you can alter your Inbox Type. If you select Important first, your inbox will prioritize messages that the service believes are most crucial to you. Your unread messages will appear at the top of your inbox. Start first to display all your starred emails at the top (you may manually "star" emails as they arrive into your inbox), or Priority inbox where Gmail learns which emails you engage with most and puts them at the top.

8. **Deleting and Archiving Emails.** When you delete an email in Gmail, it will go to the Trash folder for 30 days before being permanently erased. It is possible to hide messages from your inbox by moving them to an Archive folder, from which they may be retrieved by searching your All mail folder.

9. **Marking Emails as Spam.** You may filter undesired emails by marking them as spam when they arrive in your inbox. Your inbox will stay clutter-free since any further messages from that sender or of a similar nature will be sent to the spam bin.

10. **Making a Signature and an Out-of-Office Message.** You can give your Gmail correspondence a more polished look and feel by adding your own signature in the Settings menu. Images, links, and custom fonts and colors let you convey your brand's message. An out-of-office responder can be set up in the Settings menu as well. You can let people know you won't be available during your absence and provide them with a number to call or an alternate contact to reach out to for urgent matters.
11. **Contacts.** Your contacts in Gmail may also be accessed via a separate "App," Google Contacts. To provide Gmail with additional information about your relationships, you have the option of adding full profiles to these contacts, complete with contact information, addresses, and even work titles.
12. **Filter Automation.** If you're comfortable with the basics of Gmail, you can move on to more complex options like filtering incoming messages. Filters in Gmail allow for the automated sorting of incoming messages, saving you a ton of time in office administration. So that you don't have to manually go through each and every email, Gmail allows you to filter messages based on the sender, recipient, file size, and other criteria.
13. **Protecting Your Gmail Account and Archiving Your Messages.** Gmail's built-in security features keep your messages and attachments safe. The Google Account Settings page is where you can do things like set up and change your password, select an email address for password recovery, review your privacy settings, and even download your Gmail data.

In switching to Gmail, you've made a good decision for your email needs. It has sufficient space for a free tool, can be used from anywhere and on any device (with sufficient security to safeguard your data and privacy), and has several fantastic features that can hold their own against any professional communications suite.

WhatsApp

In order to maintain relationships with loved ones, many individuals (especially young people fluent in digital technologies) are turning to video calling apps and social media sites. Older individuals, though, who aren't as tech-savvy, may have trouble getting in touch with loved ones during a lockdown. They rely solely on regular phone conversations, which many individuals no longer have time for because so many people now conduct business from home.

When compared to other messaging apps, WhatsApp's ease of use makes it the most popular choice. WhatsApp users may not only exchange messages, but also make audio and video conversations, share photographs, and more.

We will show you today how an old person can begin using WhatsApp to communicate with family and friends.

How to Install and Use WhatsApp: A Step-by-Step Guide

We've compiled an easy-to-follow instruction for your grandparents to use WhatsApp. Once you've downloaded the app and created an account, your elders should have no trouble getting in touch with you.

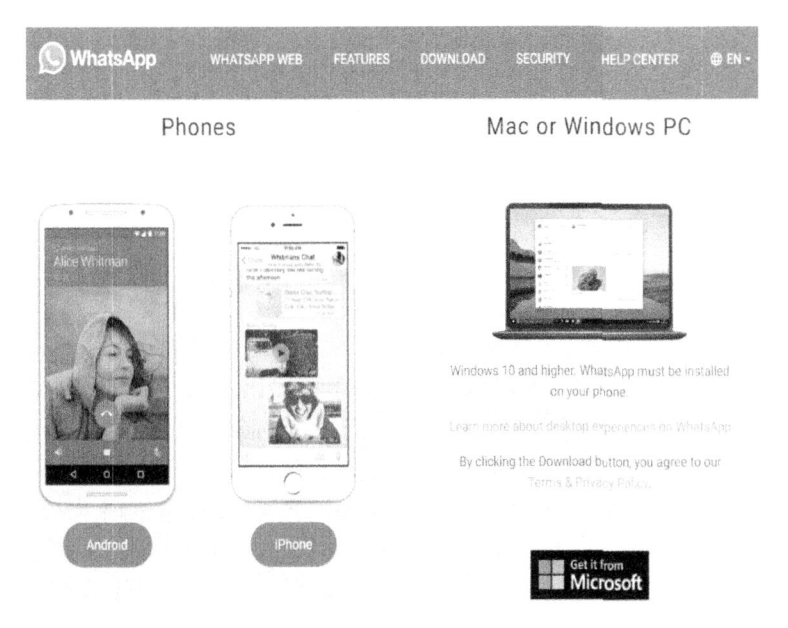

WhatsApp needs to be downloaded first. To accomplish this, launch either the "Google Play" app (on an Android device) or the "App Store" app (on an iOS device) or to the official website for PC. If you want to install WhatsApp after opening either app, simply search for it by name and hit the install button. This will cause the app to be downloaded and installed on your mobile device. Launch WhatsApp and sign up for an account.

Implementing WhatsApp

To begin using WhatsApp, enter your phone number and country code into their respective fields. After this, WhatsApp will send you a verification SMS with the OTP (One Time Password). As soon as your phone recognizes the OTP, it will go to the next screen without any input from you.

Your WhatsApp account requires both your country code and phone number.

You must now provide a Username. Either your entire name or a nickname will suffice. WhatsApp will also prompt you to set your profile image, which is optional but can assist verify your identity.

WhatsApp will automatically add the names of your friends and family who are also using WhatsApp based on the phone numbers they have in your phone's address book.

A WhatsApp tutorial on how to send a message.

WhatsApp makes it easy to send and receive messages. Launch WhatsApp, then choose the chat bubble at the app's bottom. Choose a recipient from your address book or find them using the search bar > Press the send button. The 'Chats' tab, which is also the app's main screen, is where you'll find all of your conversations. In a chat room, you have complete freedom to read and respond to messages.

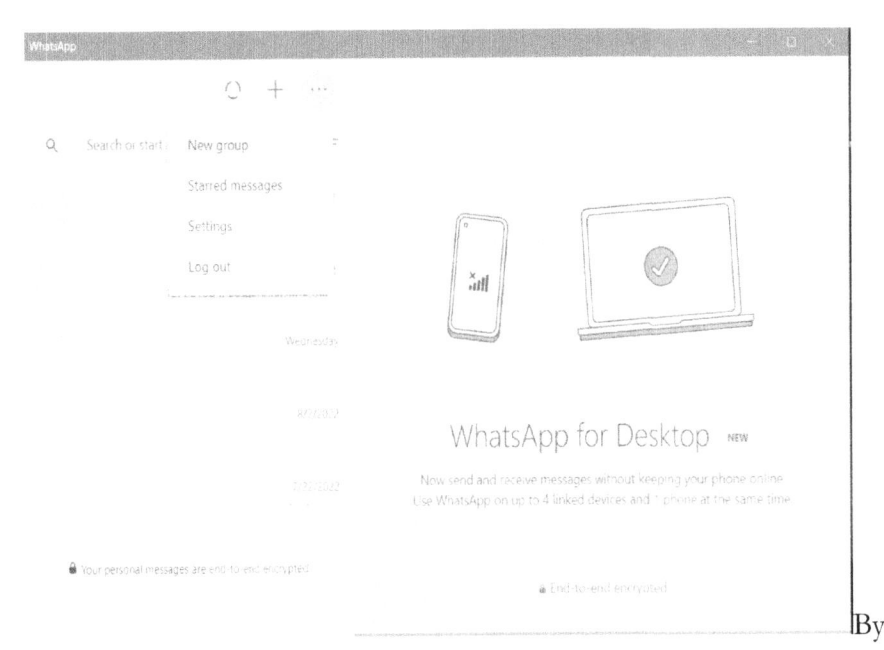

By maintaining finger contact on the chat's microphone icon, you may record and send a voice note instead of typing. Sending a photo directly to your conversation partner is as easy as clicking the camera button at the bottom of the screen.

Dialing a Phone Number: The Basics

WhatsApp enables users to make free, worldwide phone calls to their contacts, regardless of where they may be located. To initiate a call, select the "Calls" menu item and then the "New Call" button. Step two: dial the desired number associated with the desired contact. You may also enter a conversation and then use the phone icon.

Video Calling 101

WhatsApp allows you to make free video and voice calls to your contacts. When you're feeling alone, a video call is the ideal way to stay in touch with friends and family. Using the same method as an audio call, you may initiate a video call by tapping on the 'video calling' button to show people how you're doing or to say hello to your kids or grandkids.

If you want to have a conversation with more than one person at a time, such as your whole family, a group of friends, or even just your neighbors, you can easily set up a WhatsApp Group. Your loved ones may welcome you to join their existing Groups, or you may decide to start your own. WhatsApp's 'New Group' option may be accessed by pressing the app's three dots in the upper right corner and selecting that option.

Select the people you wish to invite to the group. If you want to add someone to your group, just tap the circle that appears next to their name. When you're done choose friends to add, either hit Next on an iPhone or tap the arrow icon if you're using Android. Name your Group and then click the arrow button (or "Create") when you've entered the necessary information.

Making a video conference with several people at once

A video conference can include up to eight people at once if you're all members of the same group, which you can establish or be joined to. If you have a large group of friends and want to talk to them all at once, this is a great tool to have. Start up WhatsApp > Just pick the desired Group > Start a video conference. A phone icon may be accessed by tapping the menu button in the upper right corner of the screen. Find and pick the people you wish to talk to > Use the icon for a video call.

Also, you can use shortcuts from the screenshot below:

Viber

Viber now has a desktop client available for download, allowing users to carry on phone conversations while at their computers.

The Viber desktop version is compatible with both Microsoft Windows and Apple macOS, so those who use the mobile app may continue their conversations on their computers.

Because conversations are synchronized across platforms, you may initiate a discussion on your desktop and continue it on your mobile phone. It's convenient if you need to maintain your daily messaging routine with pals. In addition to text-only communication, the program also allows you to have phone and video conversations.

Calls can be transferred to another device or held in a group discussion. Below is a promotional video for the app in case you're interested in a sneak to peek and might need some patronizing jingly music in your day.

Viber has an advantage over WhatsApp, another messaging app, because it is also available on desktop computers. Both offerings are compatible with the major mobile platforms including iOS, Android, and Windows Phone.

While you may download Viber at no cost, the purple-hued startup is probably already plotting a method to get you to shell over some cash. Perhaps it will follow the model of WhatsApp and charge users on an annual basis.

If you try to launch Viber from the desktop client, you'll be directed to download the mobile version instead. If the app is already installed on

Windows 11 for Seniors

your device, you'll be prompted to enter your cell phone number and then given a verification code to enter.

Setup Viber on a PC

1. The first thing you need to do is make sure you have the following in order to enable Viber on your desktop: Your mobile device must be running the most recent version of Viber. Both your phone and PC need to have a reliable connection to the internet.
2. Get Viber on your PC. Launch the web browser on your computer and navigate to https://www.viber.com/en/download/ to download Viber.

3. When the download is complete, choose the file by clicking on it (at the bottom of your screen)
4. When you first launch Viber, you will see: click Just follow the on-screen prompts and it will install itself. (You should set aside some time for this.) It's possible you'll need to verify that you're downloading from a safe location: click Yes\sNotes

5. Please try downloading a new version of Viber if you receive an error message stating that the file you downloaded cannot be opened or operated on your PC (32-bit).

Chapter 6: What are shortcuts?

The most popular shortcuts

Now, when you know how to use your keyboard, you can check the list of shortcuts below. Start using them step-by-step and you will see how it will save your time.

You may already be familiar with using the Windows key on your keyboard to access the Start menu, but did you know that Windows 11 allows you to combine it with a variety of other keys to launch particular apps and features? The most notable things you can accomplish with this key are listed below.

Open the Quick Settings window by pressing the **Windows key + A**. You may use this to turn on or off capabilities including Wi-Fi, Bluetooth, airplane mode, and more. In this panel, you may also change the screen's brightness and the volume of your computer.

Press the **Windows key and C** to launch Microsoft Teams chat. With this new function in Windows 11, you can start calls and meetings right from this fast panel where you can also check your most recent messages and connections in Microsoft Teams.

Show or hide the desktop using the **Windows key + D**. When the desktop is shown, all of your apps are no longer visible; when it is hidden, all of your apps are put back where they belong.

Open File Explorer with **Windows key + E**.

Windows key + F - Launch the Feedback Hub and capture a screenshot right now. This makes it simpler for you to inform Microsoft about any issues you may have encountered.

Open the Xbox Game Bar with the **Windows key and G**. As a result, you may play a game while taking screenshots, recording videos, and using other functions.

Windows key + Alt + B — Enable or disable HDR. An HDR-capable monitor and the most recent Xbox Game Bar app version are needed for this.

Start capturing a video of your program or game using the Xbox Game Bar by pressing **Windows key, Alt, and R.**

Start voice typing by pressing the **Windows key + H**. You can now dictate text instead of writing it by hand thanks to this.

Press the **Windows key + I** to launch the Settings app.

Windows key + Pause: Settings > About page will be displayed. This contains specifics about Windows and the hardware in your computer.

Window key + K: Displays the Cast panel. By doing so, you can link up with wireless displays that accept Miracast.

Windows key + L locks the computer. However, you must unlock your PC before utilizing any of your open apps again.

Minimize every window by pressing the **Windows key + M**.

Restore your minimized windows by pressing the **Windows key, Shift, and M**. You must still be on your desktop for this to function.

Show the notification center and calendar by pressing the **Windows key + N**. In Windows 11, there is a brand-new keyboard shortcut.

O and the Windows key lock the device's orientation. This stops the display from turning when you rotate your PC for tablets and convertibles.

Change the display mode for numerous monitors by pressing the **Windows key + P.** If you have connected multiple monitors, you can decide to use them to expand your display area, duplicate the display across all of them, or only have one of them active at a time.

Q to launch Quick Assist using the Windows key. By connecting remotely via the internet, you can do this to assist another user.

Windows key + R - Displays the Run dialog. As long as you are aware of the name of the executable file for the app, you can use this to open any application on your PC.

SHIFT + WINDOWS to launch Windows Search Here, you may perform web, app, and file searches.

Windows key + Shift + S - Use the Snipping Tool to take a screenshot. You can still select your desired capture mode after tapping the key, including free form, rectangle, window, and full-screen (this includes all connected monitors).

Windows key + U – Displays the page with accessibility settings.

Windows key + Ctrl + C - On/off for color filters. This function, which may be used to adjust how colors are shown to take into account different types of color blindness, must first be activated in the accessibility settings.

Windows key + V: Displays the history of the clipboard. You can see a variety of stuff you've copied, such as text, links, and images. This functionality is hidden by default, but you can enable it here as well.

Open the Widgets panel by pressing **Windows key + W.** There are widgets for the weather, OneDrive photographs, the calendar, and other items in this new Windows 11 feature. Here, you can also see news on subjects that interest you.

To access the Quick Link menu, press **Windows key + X.** (equivalent to right-clicking the Start icon on your taskbar). There are links here to the Task Manager, File Explorer, and other components of the operating system.

Switch input between Windows Mixed Reality and the desktop by pressing the **Windows key and Y** (only on Windows Mixed Reality devices).

Open the snap layouts panel by pressing the **Windows key + Z.** It is now simpler to run numerous apps side by side on your screen thanks to a feature included in Windows 11.

Open the emoji panel by pressing **Windows +. (period) or ; (semi-colon)**. With this, emoji may be added to any text field.

Using **Windows and a comma**, you may view the desktop. Once you press one of the keys, your windows are restored and your desktop is only displayed while you are still holding that key.

Search for PCs on your network using **Windows key + Ctrl + F.** For Azure Active Directory domains only.

Switch between languages and input methods by pressing the **Windows key and the Spacebar** (if multiple are installed).

Windows key, Shift, and Spacebar will advance through the list backwards.

Windows key + Ctrl + Spacebar: Changes the input method to the most recent one used.

If more than one keyboard layout is available, press **Ctrl and Shift** to switch to it (for the same language).

Turn on or off the Chinese IME by using **Ctrl and Space** (if the Chinese language is installed).

Narrator may be activated by pressing the **Windows key along with the keys Ctrl and Enter**. For people with vision difficulties, this accessibility tool reads on-screen objects to make navigation simpler.

Windows key + + (plus) - Zoom in and turn on the magnifier.

Zoom out with the Magnifier by pressing the **Windows key + - (minus)**.

Close the magnifier by pressing the **Windows key + Esc**.

Start IME reconversion by pressing the **Windows key + / (forward slash)**.

Wake up your computer from a black or blank screen by pressing the **Windows key plus Ctrl, Shift, and B**.

Take a full-screen screenshot and have it immediately saved to a file by pressing the **Windows key and PrtScn** (Print Screen, which may be spelled differently on other keyboards). Items are kept in the Screenshots folder in the Pictures library.

Use the **Windows key, Alt, and PrtScn** to take a screenshot of the currently open window or game and save it as a file. Files are saved in the Videos library in a folder called Captures for this feature, which makes use of the Xbox Game Bar (by default).

Take a screenshot of the entire screen using **PrtScn** and copy it to the clipboard so you may paste it elsewhere without saving it as a file. You can also set the PrtScn key to activate the Snipping Tool by going to the Settings app > Accessibility > Keyboard (making it the same as Windows key + Shift + S).

Open the Start menu by pressing **Ctrl + Esc**.

Open the Task Manager by pressing **Ctrl, Shift, and Esc**.

Advanced shortcuts

Keyboard shortcuts can be a much more efficient method to manage numerous open apps, whether you're switching between them or arranging them side by side. Here are a few keyboard shortcuts for controlling the open apps on your device.

Open Task View with **Windows key + Tab**. To help you choose which app to concentrate on, this displays all of your open apps as tiles. Additionally, it shows your virtual desktops.

To return to the last active window, press **Alt + Tab**. To select which window to switch to, keep holding Alt while pressing Tab repeatedly.

To cycle through windows in the order they were opened, use **Alt + Esc**.

Ctrl + Alt + Tab allows you to see all of the open programs and select one using the keyboard arrows. Similar to Task View, but only displayed on the currently active monitor and without seeing your virtual desktops.

Alt + F4 - Exit the currently open window or application This launches the Windows power menu when used on a desktop.

When the active window is maximized, the entire desktop is covered by it.

Snap the active window to the top half of your screen by pressing the **Windows key, Alt, and Up arrow together**. It will ask you to select an app to snap on the bottom part of this new shortcut in Windows 11.

If the active window is maximized, press the **Windows key and the down arrow** to reduce its size. If the window isn't maximized, hide it in the taskbar.

Snap the active window to the bottom half of the screen by pressing the **Windows key, Alt, and the Down arrow**. If the active window is now filling the full screen, pressing the keys once more will cause it to shrink back to its original size. If there isn't an app for the upper half yet, this will urge you to select one.

Snap the active window to the left half of the screen by pressing the **Windows key and the left arrow**.

Snap the active window to the right side of the screen by pressing the **Windows key and the right arrow**.

An app can be snapped into a quarter of the screen by using one of the other arrows while holding down the **Windows key** after it has been snapped into half of the screen. Additionally, if you want to transfer windows to different monitors, you can keep pressing the same arrow (still taking up half the screen).

Minimize all windows besides the present window by pressing the **Windows key + Home**. To bring back the minimized windows, press once more.

Stretch the active window to fill the entire vertical space while maintaining its width by pressing the **Windows key, Shift, and the Up arrow** (for non-maximized windows). This can be turned around using the Down arrow shortcut.

To move the active window to a different monitor, press the **Windows key while holding down the Shift key.**

Create a new virtual desktop by pressing the **Windows key and Ctrl**.

Virtual desktops can be switched between using the **Windows key + Ctrl + Left or Right arrow.**

Close the current virtual desktop by pressing the **Windows key, Ctrl, and F4**. Open applications are moved to the following virtual desktop in the queue.

One of the key components of Windows 11 is the File Explorer, which allows you to view and manage all of your files. There are a few keyboard shortcuts you may utilize to make this process simpler and quicker.

To focus on the address bar, press **Alt + D.**

Ctrl + E, Ctrl + F, or F3 - Brings the search bar into focus.

Open a new window with **Ctrl + N.** (also works in some web browsers)

Close the active window using **Ctrl + W.** (can also be used to close the active tab in web browsers).

Change the size of folder and file icons by pressing the keys **Ctrl and Scroll Wheel**. Icons are scaled up as you scroll up and down when you scroll down.

Create a new folder by pressing **Ctrl + Shift + N**.

If the current folder has no subfolders, pressing **Ctrl + Shift + E** will display every folder in the parent directory of the active folder (by expanding the list on the sidebar).

Num lock + * (asterisk) or + (plus) - Shows the sidebar with all of the subfolders in the currently chosen folder.

Collapse an enlarged folder with the **num lock key + - (minus)**.

Alt + Enter - Displays the file or folder's properties.

Show the preview panel with **Alt + P.**

Backspace or **Alt + Left arrow** will advance one page (also works in some apps like web browsers)

Go forward one page by using **Alt + Right arrow** (also works in apps like web browsers)

View the parent folder of the currently active folder by pressing **Alt + Up arrow.**

To move through the items on the current page without selecting them, press **Ctrl + (arrow).**

While navigating, use **Ctrl + Space** to choose specific items.

Shift + (arrow): Select a series of items starting with the one that is presently chosen. The up and down arrows pick full rows of items in grid-style layouts. The most recent item(s) you picked become deselected if you begin navigating in the opposite direction.

The first subfolder of an enlarged folder can be accessed by using the **right arrow** (on the navigation sidebar).

Left arrow: Select the parent folder of the currently selected folder or collapse an expanded folder.

Home will take you to the current page's top (works in various other apps).

Go to the bottom of the current page to conclude (also works in multiple apps).

Some applications have the ability to create dialog boxes that feature menus, properties pages, and more. You might be able to navigate the dialog box using a few keyboard shortcuts, depending on how complicated it is.

Display items in an active list by pressing **F4 or Space.**

Arrow keys: Choose a choice from a list of options or a button from a set of buttons.

If an item is a checkbox, you can select or deselect it using the **spacebar**.

Ctrl + Tab allows you to navigate between tabs (also works in web browsers)

Tab backwards by using **Ctrl + Shift + Tab.**

Tab - Navigate the current page's choices

Shift + Tab - Navigate through the choices on the current page in the reverse order.

Choose the option with the corresponding underlined letter in its explanation by pressing **Alt + (letter)**.

Keyboard shortcuts in Windows 11 might also make it simpler to use the taskbar. Here are a few key combinations that will speed up the taskbar item selection process.

Windows key + T: Navigate through the taskbar's applications (open or pinned)

Start the taskbar app that is pinned there by pressing the **Windows key and the corresponding number.** Change to the app if it is already open.

Even if the app is already open, pressing the **Windows key while holding down the Shift key** will launch a new instance at the position indicated by the number on the taskbar.

Switch to the last active window of the application that is pinned to the taskbar in the location indicated by the number by pressing the **Windows key and the combination Ctrl + (number).**

Windows key + Alt + (number): This command will launch the Jump List for the taskbar-pinned application in the numbered position.

Open a new instance of the application at the specified location on the taskbar as an administrator by pressing the **Windows key along with Ctrl, Shift, and (number).**

Shift + left mouse click: Launch a fresh instance of the chosen application.

Open the chosen app as an administrator by pressing **Ctrl, Shift, and left mouse click.**

To access the window menu for the chosen app, press **Shift and right-click the mouse.**

To cycle through the open windows for an app with many windows open, press **Ctrl and Left Mouse Click.**

Set the attention to the top icon in the taskbar corner by pressing the **Windows key + B**. Focus is placed on the overflow menu icon if no apps are showing any icons.

Additional standard keyboard shortcuts in Windows 11

Numerous activities include keyboard shortcuts that can be used in various Windows 11 features or in various programs. Here are some other shortcuts you could find handy, whether you wish to copy and paste text or files, refresh a website, or do other things.

Ctrl + A will select every word or item on a page, document, or window.

Delete the selected text or item using **Ctrl + D**

Cut the text or item you've selected with **Ctrl + X.**

Copy the text or item you've selected using **Ctrl + C.**

Copy and paste content from the clipboard by pressing the keys **Ctrl + V.**

Ctrl + Z undoes the last action you took.

Reverse an action with **Ctrl + Y.**

To rename a chosen file or folder, press **F2.**

F4 will show the File Explorer address bar list.

Refresh the current window or page by pressing **F5 or Ctrl + R.** (works in various apps, including web browsers).

Ctrl + F5 - In some web browsers, this forces the browser to reload files even if they have already been cached, refreshing the active window. If a page has undergone modifications but you are unable to view them in your browser, this may be of assistance.

F6 will cycle through the desktop or window's active screen elements.

F10 – Opens the menu bar in the currently open window or application.

Show your password on the Windows sign-in screen by pressing **Alt + F8.**

When menus are displayed, press **Alt + (letter)** to choose the option with the corresponding underlined letter in the text.

Open the shortcut menu for the currently active window by pressing **Alt + Space**.

Shift + F10: Displays the context menu or shortcut for the currently-selected item.

Left arrow (in menus): Go left on the menu, or close a sub-menu that is open.

The right arrow (when used in menus) moves the cursor to the right on the menu or opens a specific submenu.

In programs that let you open multiple documents or tabs simultaneously, like web browsers, use **Ctrl + F4** to close the currently active document or tab.

Ctrl + E to launch a search (in some apps).

The text cursor is moved to the start of the following word by pressing **Ctrl + Right arrow.**

To move the text cursor to the start of the previous word, press **Ctrl + Left arrow.**

Move the text pointer up one paragraph using the keys **Ctrl and Up.**

Move the text cursor down one paragraph by pressing **Ctrl + Down arrow.**

When a pinned app in the Start menu has the focus, press **Alt + Shift + (arrow key)** to move it in the direction of the arrow.

Shift + (arrow key) - In a document, start selecting text where the text cursor is by pressing these keys together.

Left arrow: Choose the character that came before. The text that was most recently selected is deselected by using the right arrow.

Right arrow: Choose the subsequent character. The previous selected text is deselected with the left arrow.

Up arrow: Choose the line before this one. The downward arrow deselects the most recently chosen line.

Down arrow: Choose the following line. The up arrow deselects the most recently chosen line.

Select a block of text in a document by beginning from the cursor position and pressing **Ctrl + Shift + (arrow key)**

Conclusion

The majority of older folks have a paralyzing phobia of all things digital. Unlike children of today, they presumably only had access to a television during their youth. It is normal for them to be sentimental and reject technology. But if you are reading this, you are aware that mastering basic computer skills is really valuable. Try convincing your parents with the following three arguments:

To Attend to Everyday Needs

Slowly but steadily, digitization has permeated our everyday lives. With the Smart Nation program, Singapore's public systems have gone online. Electronic databases now house our medical records. With Internet banking services, our money has also moved online. It is currently more convenient to perform numerous tasks online than offline. We can temporarily prevent these changes, but not for long. Consider our supermarkets now. There are fewer cashiers and an increase in computerized kiosks, however not all kiosks take cash. Everyday, our parents must learn to engage with these displays. With the prevalence of smartphones and the development of banking applications such as PayNow and PayLah, it may not be long before cards are replaced by mobile devices.

Self-Entertainment

If they reject the notion that they have "no choice," you should attempt to persuade them that it is a "good choice." As your parents age, they are likely to work less and devote more time to leisure activities. Consider: What do your parents like doing? Watch Taiwan dramas? Listen to music from the 1970s? Read about international politics? Whatever their hobbies, there is certainly no shortage of applications that might immediately enhance their quality of life.

To Develop a Family

In addition to seeking their own entertainment, elderly folks are likely to desire intergenerational connection. For all you know, your parents may be seeking your concern by requesting your assistance. However, mastering fundamental smartphone and computer skills can only increase the quality of your relationships with your parents. Utilizing social media networks is the most useful skill for this goal. 77% of Americans actively use social media. In fact, 33% of Internet users between the ages of 55 and 65 currently use Instagram. If elders can learn to traverse these platforms alone, they will be far better able to keep in touch with their children and grandkids, even if they no longer reside with them.

I hope this book could help to solve this problem for seniors.

Made in the USA
Middletown, DE
26 November 2022